D1536292

AN OUTDOOR GUIDE TO

THE BIG
SOUTH FORK

NATIONAL RIVER AND
RECREATION AREA

AN OUTDOOR GUIDE TO

THE BIG SOUTH FORK

NATIONAL RIVER AND RECREATION AREA

SECOND EDITION

RUSS MANNING

THE
MOUNTAINEERS
BOOKS

To Don Barger and Danielle Droitsch of the National Parks and Conservation Association Southeast Regional Office, for their dedication in protecting national park lands throughout the Southeast, including the Big South Fork National River and Recreation Area

 Published by
The Mountaineers Books
1001 SW Klickitat Way, Suite 201
Seattle, WA 98134

© 2000 by Russ Manning

First edition (originally titled *Exploring the Big South Fork: A Handbook to the National River and Recreation Area*), 1994. Second edition, 2000.

Published simultaneously in Great Britain by Cordee, 3a DeMontfort Street, Leicester, England, LE1 7HD

Manufactured in the United States of America

Project Editor: Christine Ummel Hosler
Editor: Leslie Phillips
Maps: Craig R. Hoeschen
Photographs: Russ Manning unless otherwise noted
Cover design: Pam Hidaka
Book design and layout: Craig R. Hoeschen

Cover photographs: *Yahoo Falls* and *Grand Gap Overlook.* Photos by Russ Manning
Frontispiece: *Big South Fork River, downstream from Blue Heron.* Photo by Russ Manning

Library of Congress Cataloging-in-Publication Data

Manning, Russ
        An outdoor guide to the Big South Fork : National River & Recreation Area / Russ Manning.— 2nd ed.
            p. cm.
        Rev. ed. of: Exploring the Big South Fork. c1994.
        Includes bibliographical references and index.
        ISBN 0-89886-639-1 (pbk.)
            1. Outdoor recreation—Big South Fork National River and Recreation Area (Tenn. and Ky.)—Guidebooks. 2. Big South Fork National River and Recreation Area (Tenn. and Ky.)—Guidebooks. I. Manning, Russ. Exploring the Big South Fork. II. Title.
        GV191.42.B46 M35 2000
        917.68'71—dc21   00-009435
                                                                                                CIP

♻ Printed on recycled paper

Contents

Part III: Other Opportunities Nearby

Acknowledgments

Thanks to the National Park Service (NPS) staff at the Big South Fork National River and Recreation Area for their support in the preparation of this book and especially for the encouragement of former Superintendent Bill Dickinson and former Park Ranger Management Assistant Ron Wilson. They, along with Chief of Interpretation Steven Seven and GIS Specialist Ron Cornelius, participated in early planning sessions that provided direction for the book.

I am especially grateful to Park Ranger Interpreter and local historian Howard Ray Duncan for spending several hours and several phone calls answering my questions. NPS Archaeologist Tom Des Jean answered questions and provided information on the history of the region, including an explanation of gravestone inscriptions. Etta Spradlin, Biological Technician, provided information on the location of cemeteries. Resource Management Specialist Robert Emmott supplied information on the biological communities, and Steve Bakaletz, NPS Biologist, made valuable comments. Former Forestry Technician Jeanne Richardson and former Chief of Maintenance Fred Kelly assisted with information on roads and trails. John Cannon, former Chief Ranger, provided advice on park regulations. My thanks to Henrietta Brooks, former receptionist and secretary, now budget clerk, for fielding my many phone calls and loaning books and papers from the park library.

Many of the NPS staff reviewed all or parts of draft manuscripts and made valuable suggestions. I'm grateful to the following for taking the time to do the review: Bill Dickinson, Steven Seven, Ron Wilson, Robert Emmott, Jeanne Richardson, Howard Ray Duncan, Tom Des Jean, Ron Cornelius, John Cannon, Jim Wiggins (former Assistant Superintendent), Brenda Deaver (Park Ranger), Sherry Fritschi (Seasonal Ranger), Lisa Collins (Supervisory Park Ranger), and Jerome Flood (former Supervisory Park Ranger).

In addition, I am grateful to Dr. Molly F. Miller, Professor of Geology at Vanderbilt University, for taking the time to supply information on the geology of the Big South Fork region and for reviewing my section on geology. I thank Charles P. Nicholson, zoologist with the Tennessee Valley Authority, for helping to construct the list of migratory and resident birds of the Big South Fork. I also thank Bob Wheeley, owner of Cumberland Rapid Transit, for supplying information on paddling the river system and for reviewing that section of the book; Joe Cross, president of the Big South Fork Bicycle Club for providing information and suggestions on bicycling and mountain biking and for reviewing those sections; Lucy Scanlon, Trailmaster for the annual Big South Fork Competitive Ride, for providing information and suggestions on horseback riding and for reviewing that section; and Conley Blevins, former interpretive ranger at Blue Heron and a descendent of Jonathan Blevins, for looking over the history section.

I am also grateful to the McCreary County Museum; Audney Lloyd, former editor and publisher of the *Scott County News*; and Dr. Benita J. Howell, associate professor of anthropology at the University of Tennessee Knoxville, for various historical photographs as indicated.

Key to Map Symbols

———————	Paved Road	●	City
———————	Secondary Road	○	Trailhead
- - - - - - - -	Unpaved Road	■	Building
················	Trail	⬆	Ranger Station
——··——	Boundary (park or state)	⇧	Visitor Center
～～～	River or Stream	▲	Campground
‖‖‖‖‖‖‖‖‖	Railroad Bed	][	Bridge
		❶	Numbered Reference

Introduction

Because the Big South Fork is a rare combination of recreation area and national river, you'll find more outdoor activities here than at most other units of the National Park System. Visitors to the Big South Fork enjoy everything from hiking and backpacking to bicycling and sightseeing, from camping and horseback riding to whitewater rafting and picnicking beside the river.

Found here also are the traces of history, from pioneer farmsteads and log cabins to the remains of large-scale development in the coal and timber industries. You can spend many hours searching out historic sites and old cemeteries or examining the influence of the industrial development that for a time transformed the region. Here, history and the outdoors complement each other, offering a broad experience to stimulate your curiosity and challenge your stamina.

The Big South Fork National River and Recreation Area (BSFNRRA) was authorized by the U.S. Congress in 1974, primarily in response to a call from conservation groups to preserve the land. The 123,000-acre park encompasses the gorge of the Big South Fork of the Cumberland River and adjacent lands. The park contains the free-flowing river, numerous tributaries, stone arches, waterfalls, rock shelters, early settlement sites, and the forest and wildlife of the Cumberland Plateau in Tennessee and Kentucky. It has long been a gathering place for outdoor enthusiasts, yet there have also been times when the area was threatened. Various plans had proposed a dam for the river near a rapids called "Devils Jump," which would have flooded the river gorge. Instead, through the efforts of conservation groups—particularly Tennessee Citizens for Wilderness Planning—and local congressional delegations, the park was established to preserve the geology and the natural communities of the river gorge and to create opportunities for outdoor recreation.

The legislation authorizing the national river and recreation area assigned the responsibility of acquiring lands and developing the park to the U.S. Army Corps of Engineers, with the National Park Service (NPS) to take over management once the park was established. The Corps purchased land, laid out trails, and constructed recreational facilities, and the NPS took over interim management as pieces were completed. In later years the Corps became limited in its activities because of new federal cost-sharing regulations on its

Slave Falls

projects, and so although some land still remained to be acquired and park development had not yet been completed, both the Corps and the National Park Service agreed it was time to make the transfer, with the NPS given entire management responsibility. The U.S. Congress authorized the transfer in 1990, and the transfer was officially recognized at the dedication of new park headquarters on August 25, 1991; the ceremony was also a symbolic dedication of the BSFNRRA.

The Big South Fork National River and Recreation Area contains two separate management zones. The Park Service manages the gorge area—approximately 56,000 acres with bare rock walls and steep wooded slopes leading down to the river—as virtual wilderness with no development, except in a few places where legislatively authorized roads wander down to the river. Only activities compatible with the area's wilderness character, such as hiking, horseback riding, and paddling the river, take place in the gorge area. Facilities that include visitor centers, campgrounds, and a stable are available on the adjacent plateau surface—about 67,000 acres that make up the rim area of the park. Here along the rim, visitors have the options of sightseeing and camping from their vehicles.

This handbook serves as an activity guide to these two management zones—the national river area in the gorge and the adjacent national recreation area on the plateau. What you'll find first in Part I is an introduction to the park, including things you need to know when planning a trip, followed by discussions of the geology and biology and the people and history of the Big South Fork; in these sections you'll find activities related to study of the area, including outings to take. Part II describes the outdoor activities available to park visitors, with recommendations for some of the best routes and locations for experiencing the park. Part III takes you beyond the borders of the BSFNRRA to visit communities, parks, and preserves nearby.

You'll find here at the BSFNRRA a rich mix of history and the outdoors. The Big South Fork is a special place with much to see and do. Enjoy your stay.

A Note About Safety

Safety is an important concern in all outdoor activities. No guidebook can alert you to every hazard or anticipate the limitations of every reader. Therefore, the descriptions of roads, trails, routes, and natural features in this book are not representations that a particular place or excursion will be safe for your party. When you follow any of the routes described in this book, you assume responsibility for your own safety. Under normal conditions, such excursions require the usual attention to traffic, road and trail conditions, weather, terrain, the capabilities of your party, and other factors. Keeping informed on current conditions and exercising common sense are the keys to a safe, enjoyable outing.

The Mountaineers Books

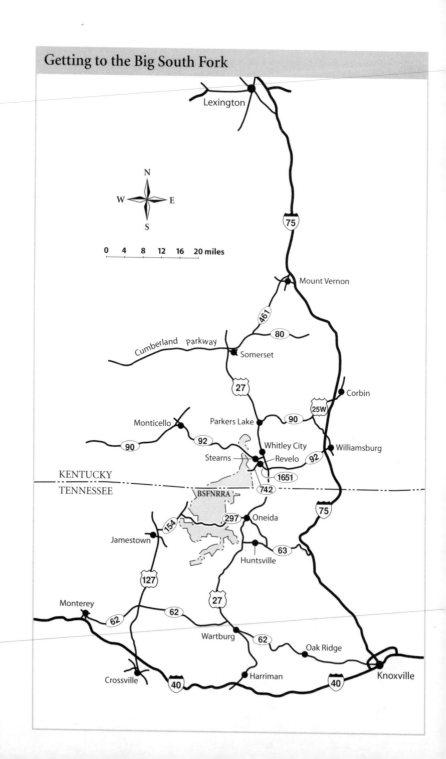

Getting to the Big South Fork

Getting There

The Big South Fork National River and Recreation Area lies atop the Cumberland Plateau west of I-75 between Lexington, Kentucky, to the north and Knoxville, Tennessee, to the south.

You can reach the Tennessee portion of the BSFNRRA by taking TN63 west from the I-75 exit for Huntsville and Oneida. Pass through Huntsville and reach US27. Turn north to Oneida and pick up TN297 headed west. You'll enter the park, cross the Big South Fork of the Cumberland River at Leatherwood Ford, and reach a right turn to the park's Bandy Creek Visitor Center on the west side of the river. The Kentucky portion of the park can be reached from Tennessee by continuing north on US27 from Oneida.

If you are traveling from the west in Tennessee, the best approach is east on I-40 to the Monterey exit where you can pick up TN62 and continue east to a junction with US127. Turn north on US127 to Jamestown; continue north and then turn northeast on TN154. You'll come to TN297 where you'll turn east to reach the Bandy Creek Visitor Center.

Farther east on I-40 from Monterey, you can pick up US127 headed north at the Crossville exit, and even more to the east, you can reach Oneida and the east side of the park by taking US27 north from the Harriman exit. If you're in the Oak Ridge area, take TN62 northwest to Wartburg, where you'll pick up US27 headed north.

Mileage to the Big South Fork from Surrounding Cities

City	Miles	City	Miles
Asheville, NC	186	Knoxville, TN	80
Atlanta, GA	304	Lexington, KY	261
Birmingham, AL	336	Louisville, KY	339
Charleston, SC	458	Memphis, TN	359
Chattanooga, TN	191	Nashville, TN	150
Cincinnati, OH	339	Richmond, VA	502
Indianapolis, IN	449	Roanoke, VA	336
Jacksonville, FL	635		

If you are coming from the north on I-75 and want to visit the Kentucky portion of the park first, you can exit at Mount Vernon and take KY461 southwest and then KY80 to Somerset where you'll turn south on US27. Or you can travel farther south on I-75 and exit onto US25W near Corbin and head southwest to a turn west on KY90; you'll travel through the Daniel Boone National Forest and Cumberland Falls State Park and then, at Parkers Lake, turn south on US27. To reach the BSFNRRA from either of these approaches, continue south on US27 through Whitley City to a west turn on KY92 into Stearns (it's also possible to take KY92 west from I-75 at Williamsburg to Stearns, but parts of the highway are steep and winding). Soon after the turn onto KY92, a long driveway to the right leads to the Kentucky Visitor Center for the park; this visitor center is occasionally closed in winter. Beyond the visitor center, you'll enter the community of Stearns, which is the old company town of the Stearns Coal and Lumber Company. From Stearns, you can take KY1651 to Revelo, and turn right on KY742, which later becomes the Mine 18 Road, to the Blue Heron Mining Community in the park. You'll find visitor information there as well. From Stearns, you can also ride to Blue Heron on the Big South Fork Scenic Railway, which operates within the park as a concession.

Traveling from the west in Kentucky, you can go east on the Cumberland Parkway to Somerset and then south on US27 to Stearns. Or you can take KY90 east and then, in Monticello, pick up KY92, which eventually crosses the Yamacraw Bridge over the Big South Fork and leads to Stearns.

O&W Bridge from O&W Overlook

Planning a Visit

Any visit to the Big South Fork will be more enjoyable and rewarding if you plan ahead. Of course, you don't have to stick to the plan once you get there; it's always fun to do some things spontaneously. But with some planning, you'll be more prepared for the kinds of activities in which you and your group would like to participate.

Call or write the park staff to obtain maps and information, using the phone number and address listed in Appendix A, or when you get there, go first to the Bandy Creek Visitor Center in Tennessee or to the Kentucky Visitor Center at Stearns. In addition to the maps found in this book, you'll probably find useful the free "Big South Fork Official Map and Guide" that shows the major roads and access points. If you plan to hike or ride horses or mountain bikes, you'll need to purchase a trail map. You can also buy hiking guides and topographic maps at the visitor centers.

Bandy Creek Visitor Center

When you contact the park, be sure to check on the weather conditions for the season in which you intend to visit. If the weather has been hot and dry, you may want to plan for shorter hikes. If there has not been much rain, the river may not be suitable for paddling, so you may opt for lazy tubing or swimming in the shallow water. Or if there has been a lot of rain, the river may be too dangerous to enter.

Ask about the hunting seasons in the fall, winter, and spring. If hunting is going on when you plan to visit, especially big game hunting, you may need to slightly restrict your activities or, at the least, wear bright clothing when you venture into the backcountry.

Once you have gathered the basic information, think about your family or group of friends who will be coming with you and take into consideration their interests and capabilities. You'll find a variety of activities described later in this book from which to choose. Within each of these activities, you can choose from among easy excursions to difficult challenges. So also think about each individual's ability. Will everyone be able to make that 15-mile hike? Will the little ones be able to handle a raft trip on the river?

Activities for Children

If your group includes small children, you can still participate in many of the outdoor activities, including picnicking, swimming, wildlife watching, sightseeing, camping, bicycling, fishing, and hiking. When out for a hike or a bicycle ride, you may want to cover the shorter and easier trails.

There are a number of ranger-led programs that children will enjoy; check the section on Special Events, Programs, and Organizations. The Junior Ranger Program is specifically designed for children four to twelve years old. The Bandy Creek Campground has a swimming pool, and both the Bandy Creek and Blue Heron Campgrounds have play structures.

Sunset Overlook

Children must be at least six years old to participate in the guided horseback rides from the Bandy Creek Stables, but younger children may participate in wagon rides. Rafting outfitters usually have a minimum age requirement of twelve for the difficult gorge section of the river but generally have no minimums for the float stretches; be aware that even at low water the river has deep holes and swift currents in places. Check with the stable and the various outfitters for suggested trips that would be fun and interesting for younger people.

Families are welcome for overnight stays at the Charit Creek Lodge in the backcountry; reservations are needed. And children especially enjoy the train ride on the Big South Fork Scenic Railway from Stearns to Blue Heron with a stop at the reconstructed Barthell Mining Camp; call or write for the train schedule. See the listings in Appendix A.

Universally Accessible Areas

The park offers opportunities for the physically challenged. The East Rim, Honey Creek, and Devils Jump Overlooks of the gorge are accessible by wheelchair. The historic Blue Heron Mining Community has paved walkways, but some get quite steep; universally accessible restrooms are located there.

The boardwalks along the river at Leatherwood Ford are universally accessible. You'll also find restrooms there that can be easily entered. In addition, the first half mile of the John Muir Trail south from Leatherwood Ford has been made universally accessible by the Telephone Pioneers of America, an organization of retired telephone workers who devote time to projects that improve the accessibility of public areas for the physically challenged.

Scenic drives, hiking, fishing, rafting, canoeing, camping, and horseback riding are other activities in which persons with various disabilities can participate. Those able to mount a horse may participate in the guided horseback rides offered by Bandy Creek Stables; anyone may participate in wagon rides. Anyone capable of hanging on can usually participate in guided raft trips. The Big South Fork Scenic Railway out of Stearns is universally accessible.

The Bandy Creek Campground in the Tennessee portion of the park and the Blue Heron Campground in the Kentucky portion have accessible campsites. The Bandy Creek Visitor Center with its interpretive programs and restrooms is also universally accessible.

Check with the park staff and with local outfitters for other suggested places and activities.

When to Visit

Favorite times to visit the Big South Fork are spring and fall, when the temperatures are mild and you have the special attractions of abundant wildflowers or a forest of red and gold. But the other seasons also have their unique charms. Winter offers better views since many of the trees have shed their leaves, and there is at times a quieting blanket of snow or an icicle-draped gorge; you also don't have to worry about bugs and snakes. And at the height of summer, you can still find cool coves in the depths of the plateau forest or take a refreshing swim in the river at low water.

The Cumberland Plateau region generally has lower temperatures and higher annual precipitation than the adjacent parts of Tennessee and Kentucky, which have lower elevations. The average annual temperature is 55 degrees F and average precipitation is 54 inches.

Average maximum temperatures occur in July and August, while average minimum temperatures occur in January and February.

Prevailing winds from the south and southwest bring moist air from the Gulf Coast that result in rains. Flooding most likely occurs December through March when storm systems dump high-intensity rains. Summer thunderstorms can cause infrequent flash floods. Snowfall averages 17 inches a year, but snow occurs intermittently and seldom stays around more than a few days before melting.

Information gazebo at Leatherwood Ford

Temperatures and Precipitation for the Big South Fork Region

| | Monthly Temperature (degrees F) | | | | | Monthly Precipitation (inches) | | |
Month	Avg. Max.	Avg. Min.	Normal	Max. Recorded	Min. Recorded	Max. Recorded	Min. Recorded	Normal
January	45.7	24.5	35.3	74	-22	14.62	1.17	4.91
February	47.6	25.1	36.7	78	-19	12.56	0.50	4.69
March	57.5	33.1	45.0	89	-9	15.26	0.80	5.81
April	68.1	42.1	55.1	96	15	11.73	0.65	4.73
May	76.2	50.3	63.4	95	26	9.16	0.60	4.21
June	83.8	58.1	70.3	104	32	14.55	Trace	4.87
July	84.8	61.3	73.2	103	36	16.82	0.62	5.26
August	84.4	60.7	72.6	103	36	11.85	0.35	3.99
September	79.5	54.7	67.1	102	28	10.76	Trace	3.49
October	69.9	42.2	55.9	92	16	13.17	0.00	2.91
November	57.3	33.5	45.0	85	-8	13.57	0.30	3.90
December	47.8	26.7	37.1	82	-18	13.65	0.22	4.85

What to Bring

The types of clothing and equipment you need to bring depend on the season in which you visit and the kind of activities in which you choose to participate. If you plan to go horseback riding, bicycling, rock climbing, backpacking, canoeing, rafting, or other such involved outdoor sports, you should be experienced and know what kinds of clothing and safety equipment to bring with you. If you do not, please contact the park staff or a local outfitter who can give advice on equipment and recommend a level of activity suited to your experience.

Even for just a casual visit, come prepared to experience the park. Wear loose fitting clothing in summer and layers of clothes in winter that you can take off or put on to adjust to the temperature. You should wear walking shoes or hiking boots that are designed to give sure footing and to support ankles as you walk out to overlooks or take a stroll along the river.

If you decide to take a longer walk, you'll need a day pack with water, a lunch or snacks, a first-aid kit, and rain gear; it rains frequently on the Cumberland Plateau. In summer, throw in some insect repellent and sunscreen. In winter, add extra clothing. All year round, a hat is a good idea. In case you get injured or lost, you should carry along a map, compass, lighter or waterproof matches, firestarter, flashlight with fresh batteries, and a plastic sheet or emergency blanket.

Accommodations

The park has camping and backcountry lodgings; check the descriptions for these services in Part II: Outdoors at the Big South Fork.

Long-range plans call for park lodges to be constructed, one in Kentucky and one in Tennessee, but they await funding and it may yet be many years before they are available.

You'll find restaurants and lodging in the surrounding communities. Check with the local chambers of commerce for listings; addresses and phone numbers are included in Appendix A for Scott and Fentress Counties in Tennessee and McCreary County in Kentucky. Small portions of the park are also in Tennessee's Pickett and Morgan Counties. The BSFNRRA visitor centers have fact sheets on lodging and restaurants in the region.

During Your Visit

Wilderness Etiquette

While you are here, take care of the park. Leave wildflowers or other plants to grow and reseed, and do not collect rocks. Observe wildlife from a distance without harassing them, including snakes, which have a right to be here. Poaching is prohibited.

Refrain from feeding the animals; feeding will cause them to grow accustomed to handouts and to abandon their natural habits, which will endanger their lives. Store food in the trunk of parked cars or, if camping in the backcountry, suspend food bags from a rope between two trees; otherwise mice, raccoons, and skunks may get to your food.

Forest surrounds the meandering Big South Fork, as seen from the Bear Creek Overlook.

Don't throw trash on the ground and don't leave pieces of unburned trash in a campfire; garbage along a trail detracts from the experience of the next visitor. You might put aside your natural distaste for cleaning up someone else's mess and pick up what others have thrown down; we can all work to keep our park clean. Glass containers are prohibited from swimming areas along the river.

Historic and archaeological sites, such as rock shelters, cemeteries, and old house sites, should be left undisturbed. Digging and rummaging around at such sites is in violation of federal law and destroys the archaeological record, making it impossible to piece together the history of the Big South Fork region.

Drinking alcoholic beverages in public areas is prohibited by state law in the Kentucky portion of the park; it is permitted in the backcountry in both states and in picnic areas and campgrounds in the Tennessee portion of the park. But the federal open-container law prohibits the possession of open containers of alcoholic beverages within a motor vehicle anywhere in the park, including parking lots.

You may bring pets into the park, but all pets must be on a leash at all times, even in the backcountry. Respect other visitors' rights not to be accosted by a barking dog, and do not allow your pet to harass wildlife.

Safety and Emergencies

Take care of yourself while visiting the park. Be especially careful climbing on rocks, hiking along the edge of bluffs, crossing streams, and walking near the river. Do not climb near waterfalls. Unless you are experienced or with an experienced guide, do not participate in such hazardous outdoor activities as climbing and rappelling, caving, canoeing and kayaking, or horseback riding.

You are expected to take full responsibility for your own safety, keeping in mind that visiting a wilderness setting in which you can at times be far from medical attention is an inherently hazardous activity. You are expected to assume responsibility for knowing where you are going and for not getting lost.

Hunting is allowed in the park during state-designated hunting seasons. Check with the visitor centers for the dates of the hunting seasons and wear bright colors when in the backcountry during that time; blaze orange is recommended.

Although backcountry registration is not required, filing a trip report with the park rangers is a good idea. Always let someone know where you are going and what you intend to do.

In an emergency, contact the park rangers at the Bandy Creek Visitor Center. After hours, you can reach the rangers by contacting the Scott County Sheriff's Office. No matter in what county you happen to be, tell the dispatcher you need a Big South Fork ranger and give the phone number you are calling from. You may also call 911. Telephones are available in the park at Leatherwood Ford, Blue Heron Mining Community, and the Bandy Creek and Blue Heron Campgrounds.

The nearest hospitals are Scott County Hospital in Oneida and Fentress County General Hospital in Jamestown. Ambulance service is available in Scott County and Fentress County in Tennessee and McCreary County in Kentucky.

See Appendix A for emergency telephone numbers.

Water

There was a time in the distant past when a person could kneel and drink from a clean stream in the Big South Fork area. But with people in the backcountry, horses along the trails, and development and farms surrounding the park, that time is gone. All water from streams should be considered unfit for human consumption. If you are in the backcountry and need water,

Stopping for water on the Leatherwood Ford Loop

boil water from streams for 2 minutes before drinking; this destroys bacteria and other microorganisms, including *Giardia lamblia,* a flagellate protozoan causing an intestinal disorder called giardiasis. There have been confirmed cases in the BSFNRRA. There are also filters and water purifying tablets that can be purchased, but ask your supplier for ones that indeed remove or kill *Giardia.*

Snakes

The Cumberland Plateau has snakes, including the northern copperhead and the timber rattler; people have been bitten by snakes in the BSFNRRA. To be safe, simply watch where you put your feet and hands, and if you must walk through high brush and weeds, explore ahead with a stick. If you do encounter snakes, leave them alone by simply giving them a wide berth. When hiking, wear high-top boots that protect your ankles; thick leggings can give added protection but are probably unnecessary unless you intend to explore cross-country.

If someone in your group is bitten, stay calm and keep the victim calm so his or her heart rate remains low. Try to pay attention and notice what kind of snake it was so you'll later be able to tell medical personnel; if you do not readily recognize the snake, remember the color and markings so you can describe it. Wash the wound with soap and water if available and if the wound is not bleeding much. If the wound is bleeding heavily, concentrate on controlling the bleeding; the wound can be cleaned later by medical personnel. To help contain the venom, apply a band 2 inches above the bite and 2 inches below the bite, or if swelling has started, 2 inches above the swelling and 2 inches below the swelling. Use something like a belt or rubber bands; do not use a tourniquet or a tight band that will stop the blood flow; you should easily be able to put your finger under the band. Remove rings and watches if bitten in the hand or the arm in case of swelling. Keep the victim warm. Ice applied to the bite site is no longer recommended.

Snakebites usually occur on the arms or legs; immobilize the limb in a functional position by splinting the arm or leg at the elbow or knee to prevent movement that will pump venom through the body. Elevate the bite site but always keep it lower than the heart to slow the spread of venom to the heart. Hike out if you are a short distance from your vehicle and then get to an emergency room. If you're a long walk from the trailhead, send someone in the party ahead for help while others carry the victim out or an individual slowly walks the victim out. If the victim has to walk out, you probably won't be able to splint the knee for a leg bite. If it will be more than 30 minutes before the person receives medical attention, then suction the wound using a snakebite kit. Make sure you know how to use the kit properly before starting out on a hike and that it is included in your first-aid kit.

Insects

During the warm spring and summer days, gnats, chiggers, and mosquitoes can be a bother. You'll probably want to carry along insect repellent for when the gnats and mosquitoes become incessant. For chiggers, you may want to use the repellent as a preventative since you won't notice them before it's too late. To avoid chiggers, do not sit directly on the ground or on a log; carry along a small piece of foam pad to use as a sitting mat for rest breaks or when you stop for lunch.

Ticks are a special problem because they transmit diseases, including Rocky Mountain spotted fever. And the small deer tick can transmit a spirochete that causes Lyme disease. Although tick-related diseases are still relatively rare in the southeastern states, you should remain very conscious of keeping ticks off you and checking for ticks after a hike. If you find a tick that has taken a bite, gently grasp the tick as close to your skin as possible, preferably with tweezers, and pull slowly until the tick releases. Avoid mashing the tick or breaking it off and leaving the head. Later, if a rash appears or you get fever and chills, see a doctor immediately; both Lyme disease and Rocky Mountain spotted fever can be treated with antibiotics.

Wear long pants and tuck your pants legs inside your socks to keep ticks from getting on your skin. If you wear light-colored clothes, ticks can be easily seen and brushed off. Also spray your shoe tops, socks, and pants legs with repellent to discourage ticks; make sure the repellent is designed for ticks.

There are also occasional hornets, bees, and wasps in virtually any natural setting; you might even see a scorpion. Give them a wide berth. If stung, treat with a sting ointment that you should keep in your first-aid kit; meat tenderizer can be used to help neutralize the sting venom.

Poison Ivy

Poison ivy is the only plant found with frequency in the park that will cause you trouble. An oil from the plant causes a very itchy skin rash. Watch for the three-leaf clusters and try to avoid brushing against the plant. If you stay to the open trails, you can usually avoid contact. If you venture off trail or encounter an overgrown trail, you'll need to pick your way carefully to avoid the plant. Poison ivy is both a free-standing plant and a vine that can twine around bushes and trees, so also watch where you put your hands. After a hike, wash exposed skin with soap and water to help remove the plant's oils.

Hypothermia

If you are out for some time in cold and wet weather, you face the danger of hypothermia, the lowering of core body temperature beyond the point at which your body can maintain its own heat. The symptoms are uncontrolled shivering, slurred speech, memory lapse, stumbling, fumbling hands, and drowsiness. Hypothermia can occur in any season and can result in death. Since the cause is being wet and cold, the treatment is to get dry and warm.

If you are wet and cold, get under some shelter and change into dry clothes. If you begin to experience symptoms, get in a sleeping bag, if available. Drink warm fluids to raise the core temperature of your body. Some people, feeling the symptoms of hypothermia, begin running to increase their body heat, but this should only be attempted in the early stages when you are coherent.

To prevent hypothermia from occurring, stay dry; eat even if you are not hungry so your body will have fuel from which to produce heat energy; and drink water even when you are not thirsty so your body can assimilate your food.

Bears

Black bears have occasionally been spotted traveling through the Big South Fork area, and a few have recently been reintroduced. They were once more numerous here but were driven out by loss of habitat and overhunting in the late 1800s and early 1900s. A reintroduction program began in 1995 with bears being relocated from the Great Smoky Mountains National Park; in 1999, bear cubs were discovered in dens for the first time in nearly 100 years.

There are so few bears in the park at this time, it is not likely you will encounter one. If you do encounter bears, take precautions to not attract or irritate them. But don't overreact—black bears are not nearly as dangerous as, for example, the grizzlies found in the western United States.

A mother bear is very protective of her cubs. If you encounter a mother with cubs, or a cub alone (whose mother is surely nearby), back off. Do not advance on the bears and do not place yourself between the mother and her cubs. If you face a lone bear, observe from a distance and then move on. Do not turn and run, which might cause the bear to run after you; back away, if you must, to avoid an encounter. Under no circumstances should you feed a bear or leave food for a bear, which would then learn that people carry food and so pose a threat to visitors that come after you. When camping in the backcountry, suspend your food bag on a rope between two trees where a bear cannot get to it.

Leave No Trace

In addition to following normal safety procedures, obeying park regulations, and generally behaving in a responsible manner, you can go one step further in protecting the virtual wilderness of the Big South Fork by practicing "Leave No Trace," a backcountry etiquette that has been formalized into an educational program by the National Outdoor Leadership School. Leave No Trace emerged as an outdoor ethic in response to the growing number of people enjoying our parks and wild lands. While most visitors to such places value the land and take care not to harm it while visiting, many overlook the details that with repeated occurrence accumulate into an impact on the land, causing damage and spoiling the wilderness experience of those who come later.

The Leave No Trace ethic calls for practices that leave the land as you find it—simple things like planning your trip, choosing your campsite to lessen impact, minimizing the effect of fires, washing dishes and yourself away from streams, properly disposing of human waste, staying to the middle of the trail when hiking or riding, leaving what you find, and carrying out everything you carry in.

Planning

Planning for a trip involves knowing what to expect and being prepared. Know the condition of the trail you will take, the type of weather you will encounter, and possible camping locations where you might spend the night. Bring along the right equipment to minimize your impact. Plan daily activities to leave enough light and energy at the end of the day to practice Leave No Trace camping.

Using an established campsite at the Big South Fork

Choosing a Campsite

While there are no designated backcountry campsites in the Big South Fork, unofficial campsites have developed in areas frequented by campers. You'll recognize these places; the ground is compacted, one or more rock fire rings are scattered around, vegetation is trampled or absent. While your first impulse might be to camp somewhere else, you will actually do less damage by camping in this already established site. Studies have shown such areas take a long time to rejuvenate, much longer than it takes to create new ones. So rather than camping somewhere else and spreading the damage to the surrounding area, use the existing site; better to concentrate the impact.

In contrast, when you find yourself at the end of the day in a place seldom used by campers, you should do the opposite—camp in different areas in order to dilute the impact. A relatively new place, where someone not long ago has set up camp, shows vegetation pressed down where the tent sat on the ground and perhaps ashes from a small fire. Such a place will rejuvenate quickly if left alone. Camping here will add to the impact and contribute to turning this place into one of the permanent unofficial campsites. Instead, scatter the ashes of the old fire and replace rocks and logs, if the person before you has not already done so, and find another place that has not been camped on recently. Always set up 200 feet from trails and water sources and away from the edge of bluffs. In the morning, return any rocks and logs you have moved to their original positions and carry any ashes away from the site to scatter them over a wide area. You can even fluff up the grass where your tent rested for the night. As you leave, turn around and glance back to make sure you have left nothing and everything is back to the way it was. Leave no trace that you have camped here.

Campfires

The most effective way to minimize the effect of a campfire is not to have one at all. Modern, lightweight camp stoves can cook just about any meal you want and cause no damage to the environment. But campfires have become a traditional part of a night out in the woods and serve as a focus for social gathering. So if you intend to start a campfire, make an effort to minimize the impact to the surrounding vegetation and the soil underneath.

Use only dead and down timber for your fire. Never strip limbs from standing trees, even in cases where there is seemingly no firewood to be found; better to do without a fire that night than harm a living tree or topple a dead tree that can be used by wildlife for nesting and feeding. When collecting wood on the ground, take limbs no larger than the size of your forearm. Anything larger will not burn effectively in a campfire, and if left alone to decompose where it lies, a log will add nutrients to the soil and serve as food for insects and microorganisms and a nursery for ferns and seedlings. If camping with your vehicle, bring your own firewood.

Fire that burns directly on the ground kills microorganisms and destroys the organic matter, effectively sterilizing the soil so nothing will grow there for some time afterward. In an established site where there is already a fire ring, you do no additional harm by starting a campfire there. But in a pristine area, use one of two methods to keep the fire off the ground. Either build your campfire on a fire pan, or on a metal plate or sheet that you pack in with you to lay on the ground for fires. Or construct a fire mound by collecting sand, gravel, or clay soil (never use organic soil) to build a mound on a cloth or plastic sheet covering the ground. The mound should be 6 to 8 inches high and large enough that hot coals will not tumble down the sides. When you break camp in the morning, smash any bits of charcoal, scatter the ashes, and return the mound material to its original place. With this care, there will be no sign that a fire was here the night before.

Cleanup

Soap is not good for the ecology of a stream or river. Even without soap, rinsing dishes in the creek adds bits of food that pollute the water. When washing up after meals, always carry water about 200 feet away from the stream to perform your cleanup. Use only biodegradable soap, or better yet, just use hot water and a scrubbing sponge. Strain the wash water with a bandanna or a strainer that's part of your cooking kit, and add any bits of food to your trash bag. Scatter the remaining water among the bushes.

You do little harm by going for a swim in the creek. But if you intend to use soap, use biodegradable only. Carry water 200 feet from the creek and bathe so that the water spills on the ground, preferably on a durable surface like gravel or rock. Much of the water will evaporate, and the remainder will filter through the ground so no soap is present when it rejoins the stream.

For teeth cleaning, try baking soda instead of toothpaste.

Waste Disposal

There is nothing more unsightly and damaging to a person's wilderness experience than to come upon human waste and toilet paper behind some tree—not to mention health considerations.

Always bury your waste in a hole to a depth of 4 to 8 inches; you probably need to carry a lightweight trowel to dig a hole that deep. When the deed is done, consider using natural wipes—leaves, moss, snow, smooth stones, all of which are buried in the hole. If using toilet paper, do not bury it; pack it out instead. You can cleanly pick up soiled paper by turning a thin plastic sandwich bag inside out and, with your hand inside, grab the paper and pull the bag off your hand and around the paper to enclose it. Then deposit the bag with paper in a trash bag; you'll need a supply of sandwich bags for this storage method. Wash your hands after this activity so as not to spread germs to your fellow campers. Tampons and disposable diapers must also be packed out. When urinating, avoid spraying plants.

On the Trail

To minimize trail erosion and trampling of vegetation, stay to the middle of a trail when hiking, biking, or horseback riding. In groups, travel in single file. Do not go around muddy places, which causes a widening of the trail; just go right through them. Bikers and horseback riders should avoid trails known to be muddy; come back another day when the trail has dried up, or choose an alternative route that remains dry and has durable surfaces.

Bikers and horseback riders are required to stay on established trails and backcountry roads, but hikers may travel cross-country, which calls for a different approach. Rather than traveling single file, spread out so no person is walking in the path of another. This spreads the impact so a new trail is not created; others coming after your group will perhaps not even notice that someone has walked this way. As much as you can, travel on durable surfaces, dry grass meadows, for instance; do not walk on lichen-covered sandstone, which may never recover from your passing.

Climbers should use only removable attachments and natural anchors. Do not hammer pitons into the rock. Avoid climbing near bird nests and sites with archaeological or geological significance. Do not disturb the fragile vegetation on the rock surfaces unless necessary for safety.

Mountain bikers should avoid hard braking, which will make the bike skid, causing damage to the trail surface. Walk or ride your bike over obstacles like logs that have fallen in the trail, rather than creating a new trail around. Always yield the trail to others. Slow down when passing hikers and, if approaching them from behind, tell them on which side you are passing: "right" or "left." When encountering horses, stop and pull over to the side; speak in a normal voice so the horses can identify you as human and not be afraid.

Horse packers can reduce the number of animals needed by using modern lightweight equipment and typical backpacking food instead of heavy camp stoves and food in cans and glass containers. Grazing is restricted; bring certified weed-free feed, so as not to introduce nonnative grasses to the backcountry. When watering your horse, use an established ford or a rocky bank where little damage will occur; do not allow a horse to water in marshy areas and along moist banks where the ground will be disturbed. When resting or camping, tie the horse on a line between trees; a horse tied to a tree or bush will damage the root system. Scatter horse droppings when leaving a camp or resting spot.

Canoeists, kayakers, and rafters should keep everything secured in their boats to avoid accidental littering on the river. When taking a rest stop, take care to not trample vegetation when walking away from the river.

Leave Everything You Find

Collecting historic artifacts, rocks, flowers, and plants, besides being illegal, degrades the environment. Leave all of these things where you find them. If you move rocks and logs for your camp, return them to their original places when you break camp the next day. You may gather edible berries, nuts, and other plant products for your personal consumption, but only if the plants are not damaged in the process.

The rock shelters of the Big South Fork are especially susceptible to visitor impact. Do not dig in these shelters for arrowheads, and do not disturb the rare plants that grow in the shade of the overhangs. You may not even camp in a rock shelter.

Pack It In, Pack It Out

This phrase has become a mantra for backcountry users. The weight of what you carry gets less, not more, as your trip goes along. So if you carried something in, then you can certainly carry it out. This requires that you plan carefully so as not to bring in more than you can physically handle. If you find that you have more than you can manage, turn around and go back to your vehicle and leave some of your equipment there.

Do not litter along the trail. Do not throw foil-lined paper, cans, or bottles in the campfire. When breaking camp, look around and pick up every bit of paper and food you might have dropped. And help by carrying out some of the trash left by others.

Lost and Found

To report found items or ask about lost articles, check with the rangers at the Bandy Creek Visitor Center or the Kentucky Visitor Center. Any article you find while visiting the park should be turned in at one of those locations.

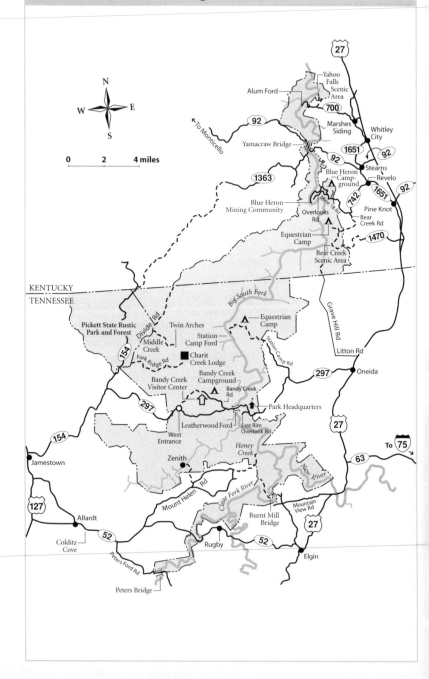

Access, Facilities, and Services

Roads still used within the BSFNRRA range from state highways and secondary paved roads, through graveled back roads that are still suitable for passenger car traffic, to dirt roads with ruts and holes that should only be attempted by four-wheel-drive vehicles. The directions in this book indicate whenever you are directed over a road that might cause trouble for a two-wheel-drive passenger car, but you should always check with the visitor centers if there is any doubt about a road; roadbeds can deteriorate over time and become a problem. Many of these are passable in dry weather but have mud holes in rainy weather.

Whenever the directions indicate a graveled road, you can expect typical problems, such as loose gravel or dirt and an occasional puddle or rock to avoid. Unless some specific cautions are included in the description, you can usually drive the road without getting stuck. But you are expected to use common sense and take responsibility for your own safety and the safety of your vehicle. With heavy rains and the freezing and thawing of winter, ruts can form, roads can collapse, or mud holes can spread. If you are not absolutely sure your vehicle can handle what faces you, back up, turn around, and come back another day when the road has been repaired.

Gravel and dirt roads penetrate the backcountry.

While driving the roads of the BSFNRRA, watch for crossing wildlife and give them the right-of-way. You'll occasionally see a deer bounding across a road; where there's one, there are others, so slow down and watch out for the next one to come across. Also watch for horse crossings; horse trails cross TN297 west of Bandy Creek Road, for example. You should always be on the lookout for hikers, horses, and bicycles on the roads.

Following are brief descriptions of the major access points in the park and the facilities and services you'll find there. Refer to the accompanying map to confirm the location of these access points within the park.

Bandy Creek

The Bandy Creek Visitor Center is the best place to begin your visit to the BSFNRRA. Here you'll find books and maps about the area and park rangers who are eager to give advice and directions. You can also get a list of outfitters who can take you on the river and into the backcountry by horse and mountain bike. The complex at Bandy Creek also has a campground with electric and water hookups for RVs and tent campsites, group camps, a swimming pool, stables for boarding horses, horses for rent on guided trips, wagon rides, picnic areas, and trails for hiking, mountain biking, and horseback riding. The visitor center complex lies north of TN297 on the west side of the river. Here TN297 and the Bandy Creek Road pass through Scott State Forest, a state of Tennessee inholding within the park boundaries. To the west on TN297 lie the West Entrance and Cumberland Valley Trailheads.

Stearns

For the Kentucky portion of the park, begin your visit at the Kentucky Visitor Center at Stearns where you can also get information about the park, purchase books and maps, and talk to park rangers. The visitor center lies just to the west of US27 on KY92. The nearby historic community of Stearns contains a museum and the refurbished depot for the Big South Fork Scenic Railway. Entering the park from Stearns, you can access the Blue Heron Campground and descend into the river gorge to the restored Blue Heron Mining Community. A trail system that leads out of the community includes crossing the old tram bridge over the river to reach trails on the other side.

Leatherwood Ford

In Tennessee, where TN297 crosses the Big South Fork, lies the Leatherwood Ford River Access. This is the primary takeout and putin for canoeing and rafting the river. Restrooms, picnic areas, boardwalks at the river's edge, and hiking trails along both sides of the river are there for your use. You'll see the old low-water Leatherwood Ford Bridge below the new highway bridge; during flood periods the old bridge is often underwater. The name "Leatherwood," some say, comes from the Leatherwood shrub which has strong leather-like bark and is found at Leatherwood Ford. Another source says that the name was brought to the region by the Blevinses, one of the early families who settled the area, many of whom had lived on Leatherwood Creek in Virginia. The river access is on the east side of the river, one mile east down TN297 from the Bandy Creek Road leading to the Bandy Creek Visitor Center.

East Rim

A half mile inside the east entrance to the park on TN297, you'll pass by the BSFNRRA headquarters complex with the main headquarters building located back from the road to the northeast; this headquarters area is not a visitor contact point. A paved road to the southwest leads 0.7 mile to the East Rim Overlook. Watch for a sign directing you to turn left; another paved road off TN297 leads to a maintenance area. About halfway along the East Rim Overlook Road, you'll pass the East Rim Trailhead, where hiking trails begin; one to the south leads to Sunset Overlook.

Station Camp East

North of where TN297 crosses the park in Tennessee, you can descend to the Station Camp River Access on the east side of the river across from the mouth of Station Camp Creek. Outside of the park, on the east side of the river, take the Station Camp Road west where TN297 makes a right angle turn at the Terry and Terry Store. The paved road becomes gravel at 3.7 miles. You'll enter the park and pass the Station Camp East Trailhead at 4.5 miles, where horse trails begin and hiking trails are proposed, and then pass a side road leading to an equestrian camp. You'll pass parking for the rock structures called the "Chimneys" and finally reach the river at 8.5 miles. Hiking and horse trails enter the area. Fording the river here at low water provides access to trails on the west side of the river; do not attempt to cross at high water. This is also an access point for paddlers and is used for fishing, swimming, and picnicking.

Station Camp Ford at low water

Burnt Mill Bridge and Honey Creek

The southern portion of the park contains the Burnt Mill Bridge River Access. Take US27 south from Oneida. At 10 miles, turn west on Mountain View Road. At 1.6 miles from the turn, signs direct you right, then left, and at 3.8 miles at a four-way intersection, right on a small side road. You can also reach this point if you are coming from the west on TN52 or from the south on US27; on TN52 turn north a half mile west of Elgin and go 3.3 miles to the four-way intersection and go straight ahead on the small side road. A half mile down this side road, bear left onto a gravel road, and then in another 0.4 mile, cross Burnt Mill Bridge over the Clear Fork River, a major tributary of the Big South Fork. You'll find parking on the west side of the river. You can picnic beside the river, go for a swim, or take a walk on a loop trail.

Burnt Mill Bridge

The bridge is deteriorating and recommended for replacement; do not drive across this bridge in a large vehicle, such as a bus or large RV, until a new bridge is erected. If you have a large vehicle, you can access this area from the other direction to avoid crossing the bridge. To reach Burnt Mill Bridge along this road from the west, drive 7.1 miles west of Rugby on TN52, turn on the Mount Helen Road, and follow the signs.

From Burnt Mill Bridge, you can continue west on the road 3.4 miles and turn right to reach the Honey Creek Trailhead/Overlook; the road from Burnt Mill Bridge to the Honey Creek turnoff can be rough but is usually passable to passenger cars, except maybe in winter when it gets muddy.

After making the turn into the Honey Creek area, you'll pass the trailhead on the right for the loop hike through the area and then continue another 0.8 mile to the Honey Creek Overlook of the Big South Fork. Picnicking is available here also.

Rugby and Peters Bridge

On TN52 between US27 and US127, you'll pass through Rugby, a historic community outside the park boundaries. In the area, you'll find the

Gentlemen's Swimming Hole Trail leading into the BSFNRRA along the Clear Fork River. River access to White Oak Creek can be found on the east side of the community on TN52. River access is also available on the Clear Fork River on the west side of the community; on TN52 after the high bridge crossing the Clear Fork, turn down left to get to the river for swimming and picnicking.

Established in the late 1800s, the community itself is an interesting side attraction; lodgings and historic tours are available. A rebuilding of the historic Tabard Inn at Rugby has been proposed to serve as the BSFNRRA Tennessee lodge, but so far funding for the lodge has not been found. TN52 will be rerouted around Rugby to prevent commercial traffic from driving through the community, so watch for a change in roads.

Nine miles west of Rugby on TN52, you can turn south on the Peters Ford Road 4.5 miles to the Peters Bridge crossing of the Clear Fork River. You'll find a picnic area and river access there. Eventually a hiking trail will follow the river north.

Middle Creek

West of the Bandy Creek Visitor Center, outside the park, you can head north on TN154 to reach the Middle Creek area of the park. At 1.9 miles from the intersection with TN297, turn east on the graveled Divide Road. At 0.8 mile from the turn, you'll reach the Middle Creek Trailhead where hiking trails begin. Continue another 3.5 miles along the road and turn right for 2.0 miles on another gravel road to the Twin Arches Trailhead for a hike to Twin Arches.

Just 0.2 mile beyond the Middle Creek Trailhead, you can also turn right on Fork Ridge Road. You'll soon pass the Middle Creek Equestrian Trailhead on the left. At 1.4 miles along the Fork Ridge Road lies the Sawmill Trailhead for more hiking trails. Staying with Fork Ridge Road as it bears to the left, you'll reach the end of the road in another 4.6 miles where you'll find horse and hiking trails that lead down to Charit Creek Lodge that sits at the junction of Charit Creek with Station Camp Creek. This is a backcountry lodge providing food and accommodations in a primitive setting; reservations are needed.

Blue Heron

In the Kentucky portion of the park, the Blue Heron Mining Community is a resurrected historic community open for sightseeing. The giant tipple, which the miners used to separate coal into different sizes, dominates the scene. The tram bridge still spans the river and provides access to hiking trails on the west side. Building-like structures depict the community as it once was. You'll also find restrooms, river access for boating and swimming, picnic tables, horse and hiking trails, various historic exhibits, and an information booth where you can purchase books and maps about the park.

Headed north on US27 from the Tennessee portion of the park, you'll cross the state line and continue to a left turn on KY1651 at Pine Knot. Make a sharp right turn in town and continue another 2.6 miles to Revelo, where you'll turn left on KY742. KY1651 continues on to the community of Stearns; so if you are coming to Blue Heron from the north, head south on US27 to a right turn on KY92; in 1.3 miles, at Stearns, bear left on KY1651, and then in 1.1 miles turn right on KY742.

Train depot at Blue Heron

While on KY742, you'll pass the left turnoff for the Bear Creek Scenic Area at 3.2 miles, and the highway then becomes the Mine 18 Road. At 5.0 miles, pass a side road on the right leading to the Blue Heron Campground. At 5.8 miles, a side road to the left leads out to the Devils Jump and Blue Heron Overlooks. After descending into the river gorge, you'll pass a gravel road on the right that leads to the reconstructed Barthell Mining Camp outside the park; an admission fee is required to tour the site. Once you get to the Blue Heron Mining Community at 8.2 miles, you'll pass the Depot/Exhibit area and the old Blue Heron Tipple and arrive at a parking area.

You can also reach the mining community by taking the Big South Fork Scenic Railway out of Stearns; when the train arrives at Blue Heron, a gift shop and a snack bar are open. The train also makes a stop at Barthell.

Bear Creek

The Bear Creek Scenic Area is one of the out-of-the-way places. Here you can walk a short trail to the Bear Creek Overlook of the Big South Fork Gorge or a short loop to see Split Bow Arch. There's also a picnic table and grill.

On KY742 on the way to the Blue Heron Mining Community, watch for the Bear Creek Scenic Area sign 3.2 miles from Revelo. Turn left. The road turns to gravel in 1.9 miles and becomes a one-lane road. At 2.0 miles continue straight through an intersection. At 2.5 miles, you'll reach a junction where you can turn right to reach an equestrian camp in 0.8 mile. Turn left at the junction to get to the scenic area. At 3.5 miles you'll reach an overlook for the Split Bow Arch just off the road to the right. Continue to the scenic area parking on the right at 3.6 miles. Another 0.2 mile down the Bear Creek Road, you'll find more parking for the Bear Creek Equestrian Trailhead with access to trails and the Bear Creek Gage Road, just beyond, that leads down to the river in half a mile (only open to hikers and horses). The Bear Creek Road continues on from the scenic area for 7.0 miles out to US27 as KY1470, which provides a shorter route if you're coming from the Tennessee portion of the park. Be aware: at one point this graveled road passes through a small creek, which could be flowing if there has been a recent rain. Original plans for the park call for a lodge to be built near the Bear Creek Scenic Area, but the proposal has stalled because of the lack of good roads and utilities and a lack of funding.

Yamacraw

North of the Blue Heron area of the park, you can continue west on KY92 from Stearns 5.3 miles to the Yamacraw Day Use Area on the east side of the river at the Yamacraw Bridge crossing of the Big South Fork. You can also reach this area east on KY92 from Monticello. The Yamacraw region gets its

The K&T train crossed the Big South Fork on the bridge at Yamacraw.
(Courtesy of Stearns Museum)

name from a Native American tribe that once lived there. The day use area provides picnicking and access to the Sheltowee Trace National Recreation Trail and, on the river's west side, a river access point. The river area north of Yamacraw is legislatively defined as adjacent area; the gorge area is defined as stopping at the KY92 crossing of the river. South of the highway bridge, look for the old Kentucky & Tennessee Railroad bridge across the river; at the time the Stearns Company built the bridge in 1907, it was the largest concrete railroad bridge in the South—575 feet long with five arches. To get to the bridge you can turn south on KY1363 on the west side of the river for 0.7 mile to view the bridge, but in summer with leaves on the trees, it's difficult to get a look; there's a turnout on the left where you can walk to the top of the bridge, but do not walk onto the bridge. For a better view, take the Sheltowee Trace south from the river access on the west side of the river for half a mile to the bridge.

Yahoo Falls and Alum Ford

Farther north, you can reach the Yahoo Falls Scenic Area by taking KY700 west from US27 just north of Whitley City. Travel through Marshes Siding and cross KY1651, which you could take north from Stearns to reach this junction. Continuing on KY700, you'll soon enter Daniel Boone National Forest and then at 4.0 miles turn right on a gravel road. If you were to keep going straight, you'd arrive at the Alum Ford River Access on the Big South Fork, which has picnicking, river access, primitive camping, and additional access to the Sheltowee Trace. After making the turn on the gravel road, it's 1.5 miles down to the Yahoo Falls Scenic Area. There's a large picnic area with hiking trails that begin at the backside of the one-way loop through the area. The trails lead to overlooks and Yahoo Falls, the tallest waterfall in the BSFNRRA. From the overlooks, you'll see that at this northern location the waters of Lake Cumberland reach up into the river gorge, backed up by Wolf Creek Dam far downstream on the Cumberland River.

The Geology

The New River and the Clear Fork join in Tennessee to form the Big South Fork of the Cumberland River, which then flows north across the Cumberland Plateau to join the main stem of the Cumberland River in Kentucky. Along the way, the Big South Fork plows a steep-walled gorge that in places reaches 600 feet in depth. The surrounding landscape is a geologic wonder on the smaller scale, with natural arches, chimneys, waterfalls, and rock shelters.

The River Gorge

The Big South Fork Gorge is the centerpiece of the BSFNRRA. From most overlooks in the park you can see evidence of the geological forces that continue to create the gorge. One of the best overlooks, and easiest to get to, is the Devils Jump Overlook on the Overlooks Road off the Mine 18 Road that leads down to the Blue Heron Mining Community in Kentucky. In Tennessee, the easiest gorge overlook to reach is the East Rim Overlook off TN297 on the east side of the river, but the rock is not exposed as much there. A better view for studying the gorge geology in Tennessee is the Honey Creek Overlook; follow the directions for Burnt Mill

Big South Fork Gorge from Angel Falls Overlook

Bridge in the previous section on Access, Facilities, and Services and continue to the Honey Creek area on a dirt road to a right turn that leads to the overlook; the road could be muddy in winter.

From these overlooks, you can see across the top of the Cumberland Plateau on the other side of the gorge. Hills and mountains in the distance, referred to as the "Cumberland Mountains," stand on this northern region of the Plateau. Even so, you seem to stand on the general lay of the land. But in fact, you are on a tableland that rises a thousand feet above the surrounding regions.

This tableland resulted from a long history of geological change. For millions of years, a shallow sea covered what is now Tennessee and Kentucky. Multitudes of animals lived in the waters. When they died, their skeletons and shells were broken and scattered by the waves and eventually settled on the sea floor where the fragments were compacted and cemented to form limestone.

About 320 million years ago, the land to the east rose. Rains falling on these new mountains formed rivers, many flowing west from these Appalachian highlands. The rivers and streams brought with them countless tons of sand and mud eroded from the mountains. This debris settled out as the wa-

Big South Fork just below the confluence

ter met the shallow inland sea and slowed, the streams fanning out to form a great delta system where lush vegetation grew. Occasionally, the delta settled under its own weight and allowed the sea to invade and deposit its layers of silt, which contained only a few shells now that the frequent coverings of delta mud suppressed life in the sea. For about 10 million years, the rivers and the sea deposited their silt and mud along this shoreline in the area that was to become the Cumberland Plateau.

Then began the final episode of Appalachian mountain building to the east that provided additional material to be carried by the streams flowing west to the sea. Geologists think the uplift, called the "Allegheny Orogeny," resulted from a collision of the African and North American continental plates, occurring at the slow pace of geologic time. The force of this compression caused a wrinkling and warping of the surface rock that created new mountains to the east.

The erosion of these new mountains occurred so quickly that the rivers became choked with the sediment. But the material eventually worked its way through and covered the whole delta area as a layer of sand and gravel over a hundred feet thick. When the deposition slowed, vegetation once more spread across the delta. But later, as the shoreline settled once again, the sea reinvaded and dropped its silt, burying the vegetation. This cycle of mountain building to the east, followed by erosion and deposition of sediment in what is now the Cumberland Plateau region was repeated in several pulses over millions of years during a time geologists call the "Pennsylvanian Period" and may have extended into the Permian Period to as late as 250 million years ago.

Under the increasing weight, these piled-up layers consolidated into rock. Water between the grains squeezed out, and minerals that precipitated from the water cemented together the mud, silt, sand, gravel, and organic matter. These became layers of shale, siltstone, clay, sandstone, and coal. The hundred-foot thick sand and gravel layer laid down following the initiation of the Allegheny Orogeny was tightly cemented, forming a tough Pennsylvanian sandstone called the "Rockcastle Conglomerate."

Later, probably much later, the area that is now the Plateau rose high above sea level in a process of secondary uplift called "isostatic adjustment." In the process, uplift occurs as the weight of overlying layers is removed by erosion and less dense rock below is forced upward by more dense surrounding rock. In the Plateau area, rain and the resulting streams swept away sedimentary deposits, nearly leveling the region; as the weight from above was reduced, the land rose.

There were several intervals of secondary uplift as the mountains rose and were eroded down again until the Rockcastle Conglomerate was uplifted and exposed. This resistant sandstone conglomerate then slowed the erosion process. Above the conglomerate, streams swept away the more easily removed rock and soil, creating the tableland known today as the Cumberland Plateau.

Some of this hard sandstone eroded also, but much of it still remains as a cap to the Plateau, covering less resistant rock layers below.

The wooden platform you stand on at the river overlook straddles a portion of the Rockcastle Conglomerate at the edge of the Big South Fork Gorge. Without this capstone, the Plateau would have long ago eroded away. It is this Pennsylvanian sandstone that has saved the Cumberland Plateau, a long linear tableland running northeast to southwest that still stands 2000 feet above sea level and a thousand feet above adjacent regions to the east and west.

When you have the opportunity to view the conglomerate close up at various locations, you'll notice different features. In vertical cliffs you'll occasionally see concave shapes in the rock tens of feet across and lined with quartz pebbles or flattened chunks of mud; these are the outlines of river channels of more than 300 million years ago that were later filled with sand. Places that have inclined layers abutting other slanting layers are where sand accumulated against the sloping sides of sandbars on the bottom of ancient rivers; such layers generally slope downstream, which is how geologists know the rivers flowed south-southwest.

Some of the cement that holds the sand grains together to make the sandstone contains iron oxide which gives the rock a yellow, orange, or brown tint. The cement sometimes concentrates in dark lines that are more resistant to erosion than even the sandstone, and so it stands out in filigree patterns in a sandstone wall.

Flattened holes an inch or two across are voids that were once filled with chunks of mud eroded from the banks of the ancient streams. Indentations and pits on the rock surface are more recent features caused by uneven erosion in this resistant capstone.

Once the rains and resulting streams had eroded down to this Rockcastle Conglomerate, the water gathered into cracks that had formed in the sandstone when it was lifted high above sea level. Sandstone is less resistant along these cracks and so erodes more easily, forming conduits for the streams of water to reach the less resistant layers below. Several of these streams converged to form the Big South Fork. Small tributary streams still slowly work through the resistant sandstone. Larger tributaries have recently penetrated the sandstone and now are more easily eroding the underlying layers. The river itself, with its large volume of water and erosive power, has removed much of the underlying rock, carving the gorge you see before you.

Although the plateau surface gave way to the downward erosion of the river, the Pennsylvanian sandstone at the edges resisted the river's lateral forces. You'll see the sandstone on your side of the river, but also look across the gorge to the other side. At places like the Devils Jump and Honey Creek Overlooks, you'll see exposed blocks of sandstone at the rim. This layer of sandstone resisted being washed away when the river was forming, otherwise the river would have spread out into a wider bed. Instead the river's erosion proceeded downward into less resistant rock layers, creating a gorge hundreds of feet deep.

If you look closely at the wall on the other side of the gorge, you can perhaps see some of the other rock layers below the Pennsylvanian sandstone—shale, coal, other sandstone that is less resistant. In most places, these other layers are hidden by a forested slope at the base of the gorge wall. When you get down to the river and walk some of the trails below the gorge rim, you'll occasionally see the layers of shale and coal in the rock walls. Rarely you'll see limestone, for only in the deepest parts of the gorge to the north has the river begun to reach limestone layers, deposited before the delta system formed.

Devils Jump Rapids

Although the sandstone at the rim has resisted erosion, the effects of the process can be seen in the irregular rock faces. In places the sandstone has gradually eroded, with pieces as big as houses giving way and slipping and sliding down the slope. Some pieces break off under their own weight, tumbling into the gorge to land at the river's edge or to splash into the river itself. From your overlook and later while walking along the river, you can see large blocks of stone sitting at the river's edge. Smaller boulders make up a rubble zone along the river. Boulders that have landed in the river cause the water to wash and swirl around them, creating such rapids as the Devils Jump and making the Big South Fork one of the best streams for whitewater rafting and canoeing in the Southeast.

Today the Big South Fork continues making the gorge deeper. If you are visiting on a summer day when little rain has fallen, you'll see a placid stream with deep green pools and wonder how it could have formed such a deep gorge. But if you stand at an overlook during the rainy seasons in winter and spring, and if the rain has come recently, you'll see a dark, fast-moving river, brown with the soil and silt and rock it carries downstream. Later while walking along the river, you'll see debris lodged in the trees 10 or 20 feet over your head by the occasional flood that comes sweeping downriver.

The Big South Fork is a vibrant place where geologic forces have created, and continue to create, a magnificent river gorge. These forces have also created small-scale geologic wonders for you to seek out.

Natural Arches

The Big South Fork region may have more natural arches than any other region in the eastern United States. The tally is not yet complete because hikers and horseback riders discover small arches from time to time as they continue to explore the backcountry. But it's clear at this point that the Big South Fork is one of the primary places in the East for natural arches. Two of the park's best are the Twin Arches in the Middle Creek area in Tennessee and Split Bow Arch in the Bear Creek area in Kentucky.

To get to Twin Arches, travel north on TN154 on the west side of the park. Just before reaching Pickett State Rustic Park and Forest turn east on the graveled Divide Road into the Middle Creek area. In 4.0 miles, turn right on another gravel road that leads 2.0 miles to the Twin Arches Trailhead. It's then a 0.7-mile walk to the arches.

Natural arches are found frequently in the Big South Fork region at the edges of the tableland surface, where the resistant Rockcastle Conglomerate slowly succumbs to erosion. Arches form at the edges of the Big South Fork Gorge because the resistant sandstone is able to support its own weight when layers below erode away.

Arches form by a number of geologic processes. One of the most common methods is headward erosion—where the head of a gully erodes up a slope until it encounters the sandstone at the ridgeline. The sandstone cap rock resists falling apart, and so the rain and seeping water proceed to erode under the capstone, eventually opening a hole in the ridge and leaving a layer of the resistant sandstone suspended above ground.

Headward erosion, probably on both sides of the ridge, is the process that created the North and South Arches of the Twin Arches complex. These two nearly aligned arches are massive; the North Arch has a span of 93 feet and a clearance of 51 feet, and the South Arch, the largest in the Big South Fork, has a span of 135 feet and a clearance of 70 feet.

Notice these arches occur on a very narrow spur of the plateau that is slowly eroding. It is likely there was once an arch beyond the South Arch; if you explore south from the arch, you'll see a gap in the ridge with a mound in between that is probably the remains of a collapsed arch. If you climb the stairway to the top of the Twin Arches complex and then climb to the very top of South Arch (you need to be somewhat agile), you'll get a good view showing the gap in the ridge where the older arch once stood. As the slow process of erosion continues, the South and North Arches will also eventually collapse, causing the edge of the plateau to recede. Other arches will likely form farther back along the way.

In addition to the two main arches, the Twin Arches complex includes two tunnels. At the south end of South Arch, you'll find the West Tunnel, on the west side. This 88-foot long tunnel took shape through the widening of a joint, where erosion has opened a crack in the rock. You'll find the East Tunnel on the east side, between the North and South Arches under the wooden stairs to the top. This much smaller passage was most likely formed by groundwater flowing through an area of weak cementation and eroding a hole in the rock. So within the Twin Arches complex, you'll find arches and tunnels created by three different geologic processes.

South Arch of Twin Arches

Split Bow Arch in Kentucky was likely formed by a combination of headward erosion and widening of a joint. To get to the arch, head down KY742 toward the Blue Heron Mining Community and turn left toward the Bear Creek Scenic Area and follow the signs 3.5 miles to an overlook on the right for Split Bow Arch. To get a better look, you'll need to hike the trail to the arch, so continue another 0.1 mile down the road to parking for the Bear Creek Overlook. You'll find the trailhead for the 0.7-mile Split Bow Arch Loop at the northern side of the parking area.

The arch stands halfway along the loop; the best approach is counterclockwise. Just before the arch, the trail enters a narrow passageway between rock walls, and then just beyond, you'll find a huge hole in the wall on your left creating the large Split Bow Arch above. Headward erosion worked its way up the slope and eventually wore the hole in the sandstone while the widening of a joint (the narrow passageway the trail entered) separated the top of the hole from the rock wall behind to form the arch.

There are other well-known arches in the national river and recreation area. Needle Arch stands off the Slave Falls Loop in the Middle Creek area. Wagonwheel Arch sits on the north side of the Mine 18 Road just before the turnoff to the Blue Heron Campground. There are also many small unnamed arches throughout the park—on the Grand Gap Loop, in the ridge above Charit Creek, just off the trail that follows the Laurel Fork of Station Camp Creek near the Middle Creek area, in the ridge above Laurel Fork, up Andy Creek from Station Camp Creek, off the Cub Branch Trail out of the Slavens Branch Trailhead, a rare double arch on land near the Honey Creek area, an arch in formation near the Laurel Fork of North White Oak Creek. Some of these are quite remote; but watch for them and others as you explore the backcountry.

Chimneys

On most any eroded slope, you'll see an occasional rock sitting on a small pedestal of dirt. While rain has washed away the surrounding earth, the rock has sheltered the dirt beneath it, creating the pillar formation. A similar process at work in the Big South Fork region creates large rock structures called "chimneys."

To view some chimneys, take the Station Camp Road off TN297 on the east side of the river, which becomes a gravel road as it enters the park. As you follow the road down toward the river, watch for a parking area for the chimneys on the right at

Chimney on Station Camp Road

7.0 miles from the TN297 turnoff. Two of the 10- to 15-foot rock columns stand on the left side of the road; they have long been a landmark in the area.

Climb up to the chimneys to get a better look. They are topped with rock stained orange-brown with a small amount of iron deposits. This resistant rock has protected the more easily eroded underlying layers while the surrounding unprotected rock has eroded away more quickly, leaving the chimney-like structures. Other, smaller chimneys can be found occasionally throughout the recreation area.

Waterfalls

Yahoo Falls

Cascading streams and falls of water are found throughout the Big South Fork area. The most impressive is Yahoo Falls in Kentucky. Just north of Whitley City, turn west on KY700. At 4.0 miles turn right on a gravel road and travel another 1.5 miles down to the Yahoo Falls Scenic Area. At the one-way loop, stay to the right and pass through a picnic area to the back side of the loop, where you'll see the trailhead on the right. Then walk the 0.8-mile Topside Loop to get to the waterfall. You'll need to visit in winter or spring when there is plenty of water; late summer and early fall, the creek that forms the waterfall can be virtually dry.

A drop of 113 feet makes this the tallest waterfall in the Big South Fork area and the tallest in Kentucky. What also makes this an especially scenic place is the large rock shelter behind the waterfall. Both the height of the waterfall and the hollowed out rock behind are due, once again, to the presence of the Rockcastle Conglomerate.

This Pennsylvanian sandstone at the lip of the waterfall resisted breaking off as the falls formed; so erosion proceeded downward into underlying layers, creating the great height of the waterfall and the surrounding wall of a plunge basin. The less-resistant rock layers that formed the back wall of the basin, being more vulnerable to erosion, began to wear away. As a hole took shape behind the waterfall, the rock above fractured and fell away. The cavity grew larger until it reached the sandstone above; this rock does not fracture as readily and so now forms the roof of the shelter.

A tall waterfall with an amphitheater-like cavity behind is typical for waterfalls in the entire Cumberland Plateau region. Yahoo Falls at the Big South Fork is one of the best examples. Another is Slave Falls in the Tennessee portion of the park. To get to this 60-foot waterfall, take TN154 north on the west side of the park and then turn east on the graveled Divide Road into the Middle Creek area. In one mile, turn right on Fork Ridge Road and drive another 1.4 miles to the Sawmill Trailhead where you can walk the Slave Falls Loop clockwise 1.3 miles to a view of Slave Falls.

You'll find other, smaller, waterfalls as you explore the BSFNRRA. There's Fall Branch Falls on the John Litton Farm Loop out of the Bandy Creek area, Boulder House Falls and Honey Creek Falls on the Honey Creek Loop west of the Burnt Mill Bridge Access, Dick Gap and Big Spring Falls south from the tram bridge on the west side of the river at Blue Heron.

One you'll surely hear about is Angel Falls, north of the Leatherwood Ford crossing of the Big South Fork on TN297. Angel Falls was in fact a low waterfall in the river, but in the 1950s some individuals dynamited the falls in an attempt to improve navigation for fishing boats, with little success. If you walk the Angel Falls Trail north 2.0 miles from Leatherwood Ford, you'll find an impressive boulder rapids in the river, but no longer a waterfall.

Rock Shelters

Overhangs of rock are the most numerous of the prominent geologic formations in the Big South Fork area. You usually cannot hike a trail without passing at least a small one, and there are many that are quite large.

Rock shelters form in vertical rock walls when softer layers of shale and sandstone below the Rockcastle Conglomerate are exposed. These less resistant layers erode more easily. The rock fractures and falls away, creating a cavity. Weathering that often includes seepage from the cavity causes more sections to collapse, enlarging the opening until it reaches the more resistant sandstone at the top, which then forms the ceiling.

These sheltered alcoves harbor some animals—nesting birds, salamanders, skinks, bats, mice, and occasional skunks. The plants growing in the shaded rock include Lucy Braun's white snakeroot, Cumberland sandwort, and filmy fern.

One of the best places for viewing rock shelters is along the Middle Creek Nature Trail. Take TN154 to Divide Road and turn east 0.8 mile to the Middle Creek Trailhead. You'll see several large rock shelters along this 3.2-mile loop. You can also take a connector off this trail to the Slave Falls Loop where you'll find Indian Rock House, an especially large rock shelter that was perhaps used by Native Americans who once hunted the region. The archaeological resources and the presence of endangered plants and animals make the rock shelters sites of special concern for preservation. Do not camp, build fires, or dig in any rock shelter; they are protected by law.

You'll find an interesting rock shelter along the Dome Rockhouse Trail that you can access from the Station Camp East Trailhead on the Station Camp Road on the east side of the park. It's a 2.2-mile walk or horse ride along the trail to the rock shelter, which has an unusual domed ceiling.

Indian Rock House on the Slave Falls Loop

The Biological Communities

The biology of the Big South Fork National River and Recreation Area is relatively diverse because the glaciers of the last ice age never reached this far south and so did not destroy ecosystems as they did to the north. This diversity of life gathers into several identifiable biological communities in the Big South Fork region. These distinct gatherings of plants and animals owe their segregation to differences in slope exposure, moisture, soil conditions, and isolation.

The Forests

The forest communities of the Big South Fork are arrayed along the slope of the river gorge, from the rim to the river's edge. To see these, take a slow drive along TN297 down to Leatherwood Ford, either from the east or west. Or drive the Mine 18 Road down to the Blue Heron Community in the Kentucky portion of the park. If you prefer to walk, choose

The ravine forest from the Grand Gap Loop

one of the trails that descend to the river, like the Leatherwood Ford Loop from the East Rim Trailhead, or the Twin Arches Trail and Loop from the trailhead down to Charit Creek Lodge, or the Blue Heron Loop, which has an access on the Overlooks Road.

Heading across the surface of the plateau toward the river gorge, you'll observe open fields scattered among a second-growth forest. The trees were nearly all logged at one time for timber or simply to make way for agriculture, but in many places they have returned to create a deep woods.

This Uplands Forest consists primarily of mixed oak and Virginia pine. White-tailed deer browse at the edge of the fields. Hawks and crows soar the currents. Hairy woodpeckers, northern flickers, and pileated woodpeckers search the trees for insects. The pine warbler and red-breasted nuthatch forage for conifer seeds. The seeds and acorns are food also for the

White-tailed deer

red crossbill, evening grosbeak, bobwhite, turkey, gray squirrel, eastern chipmunk, and white-footed mouse. The eastern cottontail romps in and out of foliage near the ground.

Then as you reach the gorge and begin your descent, you'll see exposed blocks of sandstone at the rim. These upper walls of the gorge stand bare except for a few irregularities in the rock surface that provide footholds for alum root, a few ferns, and small shrubs and wind-swept pines. Vultures, eastern phoebes, and swallows nest in crevices in the cliff face. An occasional bat clings to the underside of an overhang or rock shelter. The red-tailed hawk surveys the gorge from a perch. If you are on foot, be careful of the timber rattlesnake and northern copperhead that might lie on a rock, basking in the bright sun.

From the base of the exposed rock walls, steep wooded slopes drop toward the river. Much of this Ravine Forest was once logged, but it has revived and there still exist occasional coves of old-growth forest. The Ravine Forest consists of overlapping communities.

Exposed south-facing slopes possess mixed-oak and tulip poplar communities where turkey, gray squirrel, and opossum are attracted to the mast and thick undergrowth. The wood thrush, hooded warbler, and downy woodpecker

Tulip poplar

frequent the understory of dogwood, maple, redbud, sourwood, holly, sassafras, and serviceberry. The red-eyed vireo, scarlet tanager, and tufted titmouse feed in the canopy. In spring and early summer, you'll see the blooms of laurel and occasional azalea.

Look into the dark, shaded coves of the north-facing slopes. Where understory and groundcover are inhibited, hemlock and rhododendron live in virtual solitude except for a passing deer, bobcat, or fox. Kentucky and blackpoll warblers and the golden-crowned kinglet search for seeds and insects in the canopy.

Descend farther to the lower slopes where the soil is deep, moist, and rich in nutrients. Here you'll find the mixed-mesophytic forest where several hardwood species predominate. A forest of sugar maple, beech, poplar, basswood, ash, and buckeye harbor the gray fox, skunk, and raccoon. The barred owl and red-shouldered hawk search for the smoky shrew, eastern mole, eastern woodrat, golden mouse, and short-tail shrew.

After your winding descent, you'll level out along the floor of the gorge. Here you'll see an alluvial forest of sycamore and river birch with wild oats and dense stands of cane; beaver, muskrat, and otter live in synchronization with the river. The Louisiana waterthrush, spotted sandpiper, and American woodcock explore the wet sand.

At the river's edge is a gravel and rubble zone possessing a few shrubs. The strip is inhabited by the bullfrog, southern leopard frog, pickerel frog, northern water snake, and midland painted turtle. Deer and other large species come to the stream for water as wood ducks paddle by.

Recent floods have perhaps left debris hanging in the limbs of shrubs and trees along the riverbank. Small pools deserted by the retreating waters and replenished by rains are filled with life in spring. Salamanders and turtles grope through the sedges, rushes, moss, and reeds of more permanent pools. Swallows and eastern bluebirds flit across the ponds as they feed on numerous insects attracted to the water. Puddles serve as nurseries for amphibians that hurry toward maturity.

Dogwood

Once you reach a parking area at the river, you might get out of your car and dangle your bare feet in the water. The river breathes with its rapids and riffles, giving life to the riverweed growing in association with diatoms and algae on the flooded rocks. These support the zooplankton and aquatic insects that are food for the bluebreast darter, walleye, longear sunfish, and smallmouth bass. Mussels with unusual names like mule ear, pink lady-finger, and pistol grip cling to the submerged rocks. Belted kingfishers skim the surface, and green herons lunge for fish and amphibians.

Look back up the wooded slopes of the gorge. The different communities combine into one, and you'll see not distinct boundaries, but a wholeness and a balance reclaimed by nature.

Plant Identification

To help in identifying trees in the area, you can walk the 2.0-mile Angel Falls Trail heading north from Leatherwood Ford. Pick up a trail brochure at the Bandy Creek Visitor Center. Matching the brochure's identifications with numbered posts along the trail, you'll be introduced to thirty trees and shrubs of the Big South Fork gorge. Numerous plant identification guides are available at bookstores and the visitor centers.

In fall the forest trees present a show of color that's worth a visit to the park. The peak time is usually from the middle to the end of October. The drive down to Leatherwood Ford or to Blue Heron will give you a varied display. Any overlook in the park will present a sea of color, particularly the East Rim Overlook and the Bear Creek Overlook. For a short hike with good fall color, walk the 0.7-mile Twin Arches Trail from the Twin Arches Trailhead off Divide Road in the Middle Creek area of the park and climb the stairway to the top of the arches; if you're agile, you can then climb to the very top of South Arch for a full-circle vista.

Spring is the best time for viewing wildflowers, but you'll find blooming plants along trails and roads nearly anytime from March through October. Two of the best trails for seeing wildflowers are the John Muir Trail north and south from Leatherwood Ford as it passes along the river and the Angel Falls Trail north from Leatherwood Ford. The Honey Creek Trail near the Burnt Mill Bridge Access is also good for wildflowers where it follows the streams, but be aware this is a difficult hike. In Kentucky, you can walk the Blue Heron Loop south from the Blue Heron Mining Community toward Devils Jump Rapids to see wildflowers. Actually, any trail along the river, where it is more moist, should have good wildflowers. Do not pick, dig, or collect wildflowers or any plants within the BSFNRRA.

For both wildflowers and fall color, weather conditions and topographic locations affect the display. For wildflowers, temperature and rainfall plus slope exposure alter blooming times. For fall color, temperature and rainfall alter the peak color time and the quality of the color for any given year—drier weather causes the color to appear earlier, although with less brilliance; once the color arrives, it lasts longer if warm, sunny days alternate with cool nights.

Wildlife Watching

Glimpses of wildlife, whatever activity you are engaged in, offer a sense of bonding with the natural world. In revealing itself to you, an animal accepts you into its world, if only for a fleeting moment.

Perhaps birding is the most popular type of wildlife watching. Birds in the Big South Fork are both migratory as well as resident. The resident birds are either permanent, winter, or summer. So if you want to see each type of bird that visits the park, you'll need to come in each season of the year. Bring your binoculars, a birding book, sturdy shoes, and a broad-brimmed hat for sunny days.

Eastern box turtle

Wildlife watching can be an additional attraction to hiking and even road touring. Walking quietly on the trails, you may get to see turkey running across your path, wild pig scampering along a stream, squirrels, chipmunks, and rabbits rustling the leaves along your path, or grouse bursting from cover. From your car, traveling during the quiet mornings and cool evenings, you may see deer ambling in open fields, hawks soaring overhead, fox and raccoon dashing out of view. Along the river, whether walking or paddling, watch for ducks, fish, and water snakes; you might even see river otter and beaver.

Tiger swallowtail

Do not approach any wild animal. If you do, you will disrupt their natural activities, and the animal may see you as a threat and try to defend itself. Do not feed the animals, which will cause them to become dependent on humans for food. Simply watch from a distance, take a picture, and move on. If you are in a car, do not stop in the road to view an animal; continue on to a parking area. At night, do not use car headlights or other lights, including flashlights, to spot animals; that is a tactic used by illegal hunters.

While you're in the park, protect wildlife habitat. Tread lightly—put turned-over rocks back in their natural position, leave alone standing dead trees which are used by wildlife for homes and food sources, carry out all trash.

The History

When you visit the BSFNRRA, you'll see a virtual wilderness that gives the impression that people have seldom visited. But the park area has often contained the habitations and accoutrements of humans, from Native American camps to lumber and mining camps, from wagon roads to rail lines, from coal mines to oil and gas wells. What you'll see upon visiting the park is a wilderness being reclaimed—second-growth forest covers the land, old roads slowly melt into the landscape, man-made structures succumb to time. Yet the story of the people of the Big South Fork is preserved in the dust of rock shelters, in a few remaining cabins and buildings, in the cemeteries scattered within the boundaries, in historic exhibits, and in the memories of the people.

Early Immigrants

The first people to visit the Big South Fork region we now call Native Americans; they were here when the first white men came. But they too were immigrants, having come from the Old World to the New across the Bering Strait. They infiltrated North America in several waves of migration and cultural assimilation, from the Paleo-Indians, through the Archaic and Woodland cultures, to the Mississippian tradition.

Originally they were big game hunters. Later they developed pottery and began harvesting nuts and berries and gathering shellfish and walleye from the river. By 1000 AD, they had become farmers, growing much of their food; squash and corn were their primary diet, always supplemented with game they killed. But with a turn to agriculture, the people eventually left the highlands for the fertile and broad river valleys that were more suitable for growing crops.

When white men entered the southeast region of the United States, the people had coalesced into the historic tribes—the Cherokees, Chickasaws, Creeks, and Shawnees among them. The Cherokees and Shawnees dominated the Cumberland Plateau region, the Shawnees to the north and the Cherokees to the south. Both tribes, along with lesser tribes, used the plateau as a hunting ground, often camping under the rock shelters found nearly everywhere.

Native American trails crossed the Big South Fork region. Most prominent was the Great Tellico Trail running north to south along a ridge east of the Big South Fork; US27 generally follows the route of this ancient trail that once connected the Cumberland River in Kentucky with Sequatchie Valley to the south in Tennessee. One of the east-west trails that intersected with the Great Tellico Trail later became the Huntsville-Monticello Road that forded the river at Big Island near the mouth of No Business Creek; this road is no longer open to vehicles. A branch of that road crossed the river at the mouth of Station Camp Creek.

Besides the pathways later used by white settlers, little remains of the presence of these people because they seldom lived in the area. Yet, archaeological work has turned up relics in the sandy floors of the rock shelters—evidence of campfires, arrowheads, pottery, and stone utensils. By the time the park was created, much of the region had been picked over by amateur collectors, which destroyed much of the historical record. Today, relic collecting is prohibited by federal law in order to preserve the historical context of these remains. Each piece is now the property of the American public and should not be taken from its place.

Although you can no longer collect artifacts from the rock shelters, take a moment to stop on a hike that passes such an overhang. Imagine the people that once camped there. Here is a central place where they might have located their campfire. Over there is a dry spot where they could lie down for the night. Would they have been afraid of the gathering dark? Probably not; they would have felt at home in the natural world that supplied their needs.

Settlers

The white men who first entered the region used the same rock shelters that had given refuge to the Native Americans. The longhunters of the Daniel Boone era surely camped under these overhangs to get out of the rain and stay warm around their campfires; they were called "longhunters" because they stayed out in the wilderness for a long time. Hunters lead by Kaspar Mansker in 1769 are thought to be the first white men to have entered the Big South Fork country.

Treaties with the Cherokee tribe opened the Big South Fork region to settlement. New immigrants, mostly of English and Scotch-Irish ancestry, came from Virginia and North Carolina. They also stayed at first in the rock shelters, closing them off with leaning poles, until they had time to build better accommodations. They usually chose shelters that faced east and south so as to catch the warming rays of the sun.

From the rock shelters, these pioneers moved into pole huts with mud floors. Later they built log cabins with split-log flooring, a loft or second story, and a stone chimney. The people cleared the land for crops and livestock and hunted for wild game, settling primarily along the creek and river valleys where the land was more fertile. These were a hardy and independent people who took pride in their own ingenuity and self-sufficiency.

As more people entered the region and families grew, communities formed around kinship lines; some of the first families were the Slavens, the Blevinses, and the Troxels. Each settlement generally occupied a particular watershed because communication and contact was much easier up and down a valley than over the steep ridge into the next valley. The larger settlements lay along the larger tributaries of the Big South Fork—Laurel Crossing Branch, Rock Creek, and Bear Creek in Kentucky and Williams, Station Camp, Parch Corn, and No Business Creeks in Tennessee.

These settlements remained isolated for much of the 1800s, except for the Civil War period when many men from the region left to fight, most with the Union Army. Kentucky remained with the Union, and while Tennessee joined the Confederacy, this northeast region remained sympathetic to the Union. Those remaining at home were subjected to raiding parties, mostly posing as Confederates, but there were occasionally raiders that aligned themselves with the Union side as well. The raiding parties took food and livestock and often killed civilians. A Home Guard was established to protect the people from these raiders. After the Civil War, the communities turned inward again.

Much later, changing lifestyles that accompanied industrial development and the arrival of the automobile encouraged more recent generations to re-locate near main roads in settlements such as Black Oak, White Pine, and Alticrest that developed along the Leatherwood Ford Road.

With a little walking, you can see a few of the old farmsteads that still remain from these settlements. Start with the 0.8-mile trail that leads down to Charit Creek Lodge. In the Middle Creek area, take Fork Ridge Road east off Divide Road; after passing the Sawmill Trailhead, keep left at the fork and drive to parking for the trailhead in a total of 6.0 miles. The road continues on down to the lodge, but it's gated to prevent vehicle access. The trail starts at the upper end of the parking area. Horseback riders and mountain bikers may not use the trail; they must ride on the road past the gate to get to the lodge. At the end of the trail, Charit Creek Lodge sits at the confluence of Charit Creek and Station Camp Creek. The lodge with additional log cabins provides backcountry accommodations; you'll need to make reservations prior to going if you want to spend the night.

The main lodge structure at Charit Creek incorporates an old log cabin said by some to be the homeplace of Jonathan Blevins, one of the earliest settlers of the region. Born in Virginia in 1779, he first moved with his parents to North Carolina before they made a final move to Kentucky in the late 1700s. According to a Blevins family genealogy study, Jonathan Blevins settled in the Bell Farm area along Rock Creek to the northwest of the park and then moved into the Scott County area of Tennessee sometime between 1850 and 1860. Some say he first settled on No Business Creek, but he ended up living on Station Camp Creek, perhaps at the site of the lodge, but also perhaps farther down the creek near where he is buried.

The original log cabin, which is now part of Charit Creek Lodge, was erected sometime before Jonathan Blevins arrived, probably around 1816; it's not known by whom. The oldest part of the house is the one-room log cabin with chimney that's the far west part of the lodge. Another room was added later, almost as a separate cabin but with the chimney in the middle connecting the two, creating what's called a "saddlebag" cabin. The comparatively rough-hewn logs of the addition indicates that different people probably built the two portions of the cabin.

In 1803, Blevins married Katy Troxel, the daughter of Jacob Troxel and Cornblossom, the daughter of the Cherokee Chief Chuqualatague, or "Doublehead." Troxel had been sent into the region during the American Revolution to befriend the Cherokees and help ensure they did not side with the British. He was called "Big Jake" because he stood over six feet tall. After becoming enamored with the chief's daughter, he married her and stayed in the region until his death in 1810. An official U.S. Army headstone erected at the KY700 turnoff to the Yahoo Falls Scenic Area marks the gen-

John Blevins barn at Charit Creek Lodge
(Courtesy of Audney Lloyd)

eral location where some of his descendants think he was buried. Other accounts say he left the region and died later in Alabama.

Katy Troxel died in 1813 or 1814. After his first wife's death, Jonathan Blevins married Sarah Minton. When he brought his family to Station Camp, the family may have still included several children. Blevins died in 1863 from bee stings and is buried in the Hatfield Cemetery about 2 miles below the lodge on Station Camp Creek.

Later, others lived at Charit Creek—Jonathan Burke and William Riley Hatfield, both of whom lie in a small cemetery above the lodge stables. Later, John Blevins, a great-grandson of Jonathan Blevins, lived there. Around 1930, he and his son, Oscar, built the four-crib barn of hand-hewn hemlock and oak logs that's located near the lodge; they followed the design of the original barn that had burned. John Blevins, again probably with Oscar, also built the hand-hewn log corncrib that stands in front of the lodge and the rived-log blacksmith shop behind the lodge. The last family to live there, the Phillips, sold the homesite to Joe Simpson around 1963; he operated it as the Parch Corn Hunting Lodge until 1982, when the U.S. Army Corps of Engineers purchased it for the park. Simpson brought in logs from other houses in the area to create the two smaller cabins that now serve as bunkhouses. One was the Jacob Blevins Jr. cabin from up Station Camp Creek and the other was the Appalonia Slaven cabin from farther down creek, also called the Ellen Place for the wife of Daniel Blevins; they were early residents. Logs from a house Simpson found in Slagle Hollow, Kentucky, now make up the east end of the main lodge building. A newer barn to the east side of the complex that was erected by Simpson now serves as the horse stable.

After the complex became part of the BSFNRRA, it was renamed Charit Creek, after the creek that flows beside it. At first it operated as a youth hostel, but it then became a lodge for the general public.

Station Camp Creek, which flows in front of the lodge, was so named because it was a gathering place for early longhunters, or some say a place where militia took station. The camp was probably established by hunters from the Watauga Settlement, the first settlement in what was to become the state of Tennessee.

The longhunters and their descendants settled the valley along the creek so that by 1850 there were 126 people living on subsistence farms in the valley. In the 1930s, Station Camp still had a post office. Nothing of the community remains now except a few small cemeteries and the old cabin and outbuildings at Charit Creek Lodge.

The far bunkhouse cabin within the lodge complex was built with logs from the Jacob Blevins Jr. homeplace. You can get to Jakes Place by walking the Twin Arches/Charit Creek Loop clockwise from Charit Creek 1.4 miles. The homesite may date to the same time that the old cabin at Charit Creek Lodge was built. But it was in 1884 that Jacob Blevins Jr. brought his new wife, Viannah ("Vie") West, here to a log cabin he built in the early 1880s. A grandson of Jonathan Blevins and Katy Troxel, Jacob Jr. was known as "Jakey" and as "Uncle Jake" in later years. He and his wife raised nine children at their homestead, including the John Blevins who later lived at the Charit Creek Lodge site. Jakey died in 1935, followed a decade later by Vie. Jakes Place was marked by a solitary stone chimney; today you'll find a line of rocks where it was pushed over to dismantle it, a forlorn place.

To continue the history of the Blevins family, walk the Oscar Blevins Farm Loop. You can pick up a pamphlet guide to the trail at the Bandy Creek Visitor Center and then make your

Jacob Blevins Jr.
(Courtesy of Audney Lloyd)

way to the Bandy Creek Trailhead, which is just west of the visitor center. About halfway along the 3.6-mile loop, you'll reach the Oscar Blevins Farm. An open field spreads out from a large barn flanked by a log house and outbuildings that include a corncrib; to the front stands a more modern frame house. The farm, a historic site representative of early 20th century homesteads in the region, was the home of Oscar and Martha Ermon Blevins; Oscar was a great-great grandson of Jonathan Blevins.

After growing up on Station Camp Creek, Oscar Blevins moved to this location with his new wife, Ermon, in 1940; they later had a son, Lawrence. They first lived in the older log house to the rear that had been built in 1879 by John B. Blevins, Oscar's great uncle and a brother to Jacob Blevins Jr. For the two-room, story and a half structure, hewn logs were used to construct the east room and sawn timbers were used for the west room, which was probably a later addition. The corncrib is another older structure, built of hewn logs around the same time as the log house.

Oscar and Ermon later built the more modern house that's part of the farmstead in a style typical of the region called the "Cumberland House." The characteristic layout is one and a half stories, two rooms wide and one or two rooms deep, two front doors with a long front porch, and perhaps a later addition. Such houses usually have a central chimney; the Blevins house, though, has two chimneys. The Blevins house is three rooms across, but still has the characteristic two front doors. The Cumberland House is wood frame construction, typically clapboard or covered with rolled asphalt. The design of the Cumberland House could have simply been a variation on the saddle-

John B. Blevins log house at the Oscar Blevins farm site
(Courtesy of Benita J. Howell)

bag log cabin, an improvement that occurred once different building materials became available. But it may be that the design was introduced to the region; the Cumberland House was among the types of houses found in coal camps around 1900.

The Blevinses moved into their new Cumberland House in 1950. The smokehouse behind the home was also built around 1950. Oscar Blevins built the large barn to the rear in 1963. In that more modern age, the Blevinses chose to continue to live a subsistence life-style as their ancestors had, independent and self-sufficient.

Oscar and Ermon Blevins still lived on their farm at the time the national river and recreation area was formed. They moved from their house to make way for the public park. They settled on Peters Ford Road to the south in 1979; Oscar died in 1988.

You can also see the Oscar Blevins Farm by continuing along the Bandy Creek Road another 2.4 miles beyond the Bandy Creek Trailhead; the road becomes gravel. A short gravel road to the left leads down to the farm.

Along the main road, before reaching the turn to the Oscar Blevins farm site, you'll pass the Lora E. Blevins Farmstead. The Blevins House is a story and a half, two-room log home built in 1927 by Lora Blevins. Blevins and his wife, Tealie Slavy, raised several children here; he had come from the Station Camp East area and she from No Business Creek. These were a different line of Blevinses from Oscar Blevins' side of the family.

Although sawmill lumber was available at the time, Lora Blevins chose to build a log house, probably because it was inexpensive; he used trees from his own property, which were relatively small since most large trees had already been cut down by then. The original porches and a shed addition to the house are missing; an original stone chimney was replaced with the existing concrete-block chimney around 1967. The site also has a story and a half, double-crib barn of partially hewn logs completed by Lora Blevins in the 1930s. You'll also see a single-pen log corncrib with a frame porch added along the front and a vertical plank shed added to one side, built about the same time. Next to the house stands a small well house with the well casing still protruding from the ground. A smokehouse that stood on the other side of the main house is now gone.

Adjacent to the Lora E. Blevins Site lies the Katie Blevins Cemetery, where you can wander through the gravesites of some of the early settlers. Both Jacob Jr. and Vie Blevins are buried here. Jakey's father, Jacob Blevins, the son of Jonathan and Katy Troxel and named for his grandfather, Jacob Troxel, was the first to be buried in the cemetery along with his wife Catherine, who was known as "Katie" or "Katy." Lora Blevins is also buried here.

Katie Blevins Cemetery

Oscar and Ermon (Martha E.) Blevins are buried here too, along with Oscar's father, John, and his mother, Louise. Also look for the grave of Calvin Blevins, the brother of Oscar Blevins. Notice a different name at the foot of the grave. Local people tell the story of how one night Calvin killed a man with a shot meant to scare a group away from fish traps that Blevins and some friends had placed in the river. One side of the story says the shot glanced off a tree and into one of the men. To avoid possible retribution from the man's family and perhaps being forced into having to defend himself, and also perhaps afraid of what the law would think, Blevins left the area and joined the army under the name of John R. Phillips. Years later, he returned to the region to live out his days, maintaining his false name, although most people knew who he was. When he died in 1984, the U.S. Army honored his service with the plaque that bears the Phillips name, while his family laid the headstone that bears his real name.

Exploring the Katie Blevins Cemetery, you'll find the graves of other Blevinses and those of the Slavens who were another prominent family. Some of the gravestones have the pictures of those buried. You can see Viannah Blevins, but Jakey's picture is gone. You can see on gravestones the likenesses of John and Elvira Litton, members of another of the Big South Fork families. The Litton farm and home also lie near the Bandy Creek area. The site rests along a 5.9-mile loop trail. You can take a connector trail from the Bandy Creek Trailhead, or you can drive into the campground and park near the swimming pool to access the trail. The farm is about halfway along the loop.

The farmstead sits in a cove with John Litton's log cabin, built around 1900, commanding the valley. Below the house, an earthen dam holds a stream-fed pond still alive with fish. In the trees above the pond are rockhouses once enclosed with wooden rails where the family kept livestock. Sitting in the meadow, an English-style barn has a first story built of hewn logs and a second story of oak plank walls; its drivethrough is located on the side instead of the gable end. Built by Litton around 1900, the barn may have been assembled from more than one original building. The Littons raised several children on this farmstead. John Litton died in 1935 and his wife, Vi, in 1945.

John Litton

The Litton Farm is also referred to as the "General Slaven Farm." "General" was his name, not a military title. The Slavens were the only other family to live here; they added a wraparound frame addition on the west and south sides and a porch on the north and east sides.

John Litton was known as a master cabin builder and built several in the park, including a cabin for Armstead Blevins on Parch Corn Creek in 1881. The structure was a story and a half, single pen, log house. This cabin burned in 1998; only the chimney remains. You can reach the cabin site by hiking the John Muir Trail north into the backcountry from Leatherwood Ford or taking the horse trail north from Station Camp Creek. Continuing on these trails north of

Parch Corn Creek, you'll enter the site of the old community around No Business Creek where about 125 people once lived. It was a community similar to that at Station Camp Creek to the south. Now you'll only find a few building and house foundations and chimney remains. No Business Creek got its name, as one story goes, when a lone couple first tried to settle the watershed; the wife said they had no business leaving home and no business trying to stay here.

By the time the national river and recreation area was authorized in 1974, there were only about forty households of year-round residents still living within the proposed boundaries. Their lands were purchased for the establishment of the park.

Cemeteries

Perhaps the most obvious reminders of the pioneers and farmers that once settled the Big South Fork are their cemeteries. There are now fifty-four cemeteries or grave sites known within the BSFNRRA. Hiking or riding the backcountry, you'll occasionally come upon single grave sites or a gathering of a few headstones. If you find one of these while exploring the backcountry, you might note the location and any inscriptions that are legible on the headstones and report to the rangers to make sure the site is one that is already known.

In addition, there are a number of larger cemetery plots where small communities once flourished. Many of these are maintained by descendants who still live in the area. If you're interested in the history of the region, it's fun to study the gravestones, tracing the lineage of the Big South Fork families, among them the Blevinses, Slavens, Troxels, Phillips, Waters, Roysdens, Watsons, Spradlins, Kings, Dolens, Boyatts, and Ledbetters. For information on family histories and gravesites, you might contact the local county historical societies.

When the first of the pioneers who came to the area died, they were buried by their peers in a style consistent with 18th-century European burials; a grave was often covered with a coffin-shaped monolith or at times an arched stone crypt, which might be slabs of stone leaning against each other to form a roof over the grave. These capstones or crypts usually had the

Cemeteries and gravesites lie within the park boundaries.

name of the deceased and date of birth and death inscribed.

Later generations seem to have lost this attachment to European burial traditions and so later graves are marked simply with inscribed head and foot stones of hand-hewn sandstone or limestone. With time and in the isolation of the Big South Fork country, there was a deterioration of literacy and so grammatical and spelling errors and reversed letters began to appear in the inscriptions. Some simply had the initials of the deceased and the dates of birth and death. From 1900 to the late 1920s, illiteracy was common, and gravestone inscriptions virtually disappeared; many graves were marked by unshaped fieldstones rather than shaped headstones.

When the coal and timber industries came to the region, education was brought back to the Big South Fork. Graves from the late 1920s and early 1930s possess gravestones with inscriptions, showing an increase in literacy. In later years, inscribed gravestones of sandstone, limestone, concrete, and imported marble followed the cultural norm for the wider region.

You might find at a few cemeteries a form of roofed protection for a grave; called a "grave house," it usually consists of a roof on posts over the gravesite. Many of the cemeteries also have benches to one side for graveside and memorial services.

The Park Service maintains access to cemeteries for those who have family buried within the boundaries of the BSFNRRA. Within the adjacent area, cemeteries can be reached with existing improved roads. Access to cemeteries in the gorge area is limited to existing roads and trails maintained at the same level as when the land was turned over to the Park Service. You can at any time hike a trail into the gorge to visit a cemetery. But if you have family in a gorge cemetery and wish to visit using an existing road that is now closed to vehicular traffic, you may arrange to use the road by contacting the Chief Ranger at the park headquarters.

Cemeteries in the Big South Fork

Cemetery	Directions
1 **Katie Blevins Cemetery**	At the Lora E. Blevins Historic Site; take the Bandy Creek Road west 0.8 mile from the visitor center.
2 **Hattie Blevins Cemetery**	In the Middle Creek area; take the left fork off Divide Road at Three Forks 4.7 miles from TN154.

Cemeteries in the Big South Fork

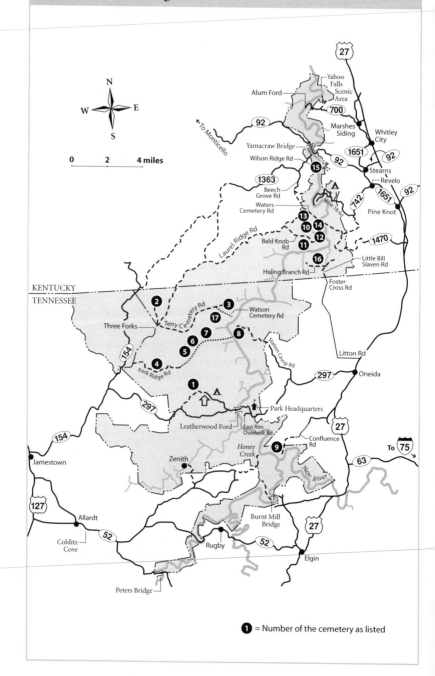

1 = Number of the cemetery as listed

❸ Terry Cemetery

In the Middle Creek area; take the right fork at Three Forks, 0.2 mile beyond the turnoff for the Hattie Blevins Cemetery; the improved road ends just beyond cemetery at 5.7 miles.

❹ Dirt Rockhouse Cemetery

In the Middle Creek area; stay left on Fork Ridge Road, after the Sawmill Trailhead 1.4 miles from Divide Road, and then in 0.2 mile take the first road left into the cemetery.

❺ Charit Creek Cemetery

Above the stables at Charit Creek Lodge; take Fork Ridge Road all the way to the parking area 4.6 miles beyond the Sawmill Trailhead and hike (0.8 mile) or ride horses or mountain bikes (1.5 miles) down to the lodge.

❻ Hatfield Cemetery

Along Station Camp Creek; follow the Station Camp Creek Trail from the Charit Creek Lodge 1.7 miles east.

❼ Owens Cemetery

Along Station Camp Creek; follow the Station Camp Creek Trail another half mile east from the Hatfield Cemetery.

❽ Slaven Cemetery

Near Chimney Rocks; take Station Camp Road from TN297 7.0 miles and turn left just beyond Chimney Rocks to the cemetery.

❾ Dewey-Phillips Cemetery

South of Oneida on US27, follow the directions given in the section on paddling to the road that leads to the confluence behind the airport. The cemetery is on the right, just before parking at the end of Confluence Road.

⑩ King Cemetery

Near the Ledbetter Place Trailhead; 7.2 miles along Beech Grove Road from KY1363, take Bald Knob Road south 1.4 miles to the trailhead to park and then walk back up the road to where the KY Trail heads northeast off the road; follow the trail 0.2 mile up to the cemetery.

⑪ Hill Cemetery

Near the Ledbetter Place Trailhead; from the trailhead, continue down the Bald Knob road 0.2 mile to where an old road leads right with the cemetery just up this side road on your right.

⑫ Newt King Cemetery

At the end of Bald Knob Road; continue down the road from the Hill Cemetery turnoff 0.9 mile to end of road and cemetery up to left; this road has been improved but could still have a mud puddle or two after a rain and there's a steep section with loose gravel toward the end that might also be muddy.

⑬ Barr Cemetery

Near Beech Grove Church; turn east off Beech Grove Road on the Waters Cemetery Road just west of Beech Grove Church or a half mile before the Bald Knob Road; this road is also used as a horse trail; you'll find the cemetery on the right in 0.3 mile where a road turns left leading to parking for the Dick Gap Overlook.

⑭ Waters Cemetery

Near Beech Grove Church; continue down the Waters Cemetery Road from the Barr Cemetery to the road's end and the cemetery in one mile; just before the cemetery, the road splits in a turnaround, so go either way; another steep section of road leads from the turnaround to the cemetery; although this road has been improved, there could be a mud puddle or two after a rain.

⑮ Wilson Cemetery

Before the Beech Grove community; 1.4 miles from KY1363 on the way to Beech Grove community and Bald Knob Road, turn left on the graveled Wilson Ridge Road; at 2.9 miles from the beginning of Wilson Ridge Road, turn right up a small gravel road to the cemetery; on the way to the Wilson Cemetery, at 0.7 mile from the beginning of Wilson Ridge Road, you'll pass the large Nancy Graves Cemetery that's outside the park boundary.

⑯ Dolen-Musgrove Cemetery

At the Foster Cross Road Baptist Church, turn right to take the graveled Foster Cross Road 1.0 mile down to cross the Kentucky state line and also the boundary of the BSFNRRA onto Little Bill Slaven Road, headed toward the Slaven Branch Trailhead (see directions in horseback riding section); at 2.2 miles, the Huling Branch Road turns left, and just beyond, a second road on the left leads to the cemetery.

⑰ Watson-Pennington Cemetery

On Terry Cemetery Loop; at 5.2 miles along Terry Cemetery Road, the horse route turns right on the Watson Cemetery Road. A single vehicle can park beside the road that leads 1.5 miles to the cemetery.

Industrial Development

The era of pioneer settlements and subsistence farms lasted from the time Jonathan Blevins entered the region until his descendent Oscar Blevins and his wife Ermon moved away from their Big South Fork homestead to make way for the park. During this period, a new era of resource extraction began and then ran simultaneously with the farming communities.

The extractive industry started around 1812, when mining for saltpeter in the rock shelters of the Big South Fork helped to supply an essential ingredient for gun powder used in the War of 1812. Potassium nitrate, the chemical name of saltpeter, is found in the sandstone cliffs and rock walls and the floors of rock shelters. The saltpeter results from the decay of vegetation which releases nitrates that then leach down through the rock to collect at impermeable layers or soak into the soil of the shelter floors. Droppings from bats that take shelter in the rock overhangs added to the nitrates in the shelter floors. The miners would blast rock from the walls and collect debris and soil from the rock shelters and put them in large vats. The miners then poured boiling water over the rock and soil to dissolve the potassium nitrate. If the nitrate was a calcium nitrate, the solution would have to be mixed with a potassium-

Coal-mining in the Big South Fork area
(Courtesy of Stearns Museum)

containing solution, which the miners produced by pouring water over wood ash; the potassium would take the place of the calcium. With filtering and boiling of the liquid that drained from the bottom of the vats, the miners had saltpeter crystals.

The commercial phase of the extractive industry perhaps began with the discovery of oil in 1818, although oil was not the objective. In 1817, Marcus Huling and Andrew Zimmerman searched the Big South Fork country for a site to drill for salt, much sought after for use as a preservative in a time before refrigeration. They settled on a tract of land on the west side of the Big South Fork in Kentucky that they leased from Martin Beaty, who had recently purchased the land with the hope of beginning salt production.

After drilling to a depth of more than 200 feet using a spring-pole rig they operated with their feet, Huling and Zimmerman struck oil rather than the salt-laden water they had hoped for. Unfortunately for the men, oil at the time was virtually worthless. Zimmerman gave up the operation and left the area, but Huling remained, determined to make back his investment by finding some use for the oil. He first tried to get his oil out of the wilderness by hiring men to take a dugout canoe downriver with a couple of barrels of oil lashed to it. The canoe wrecked at the Devils Jump Rapids downstream, and the casks were thrown against boulders and burst open. That is perhaps how the rapids got its name; the locals called the oil "Devil's Tar" and said the Devil had reclaimed his property at the rapids. But the name probably comes from the men who later rode rafts of logs downriver as a way of getting timber out of the river gorge; because of the danger of riding the rafts, the men were called "devils." These daredevils would jump from their rafts when they approached this particularly difficult rapid.

After the failure of river transport for the oil, Huling managed to haul casks of the oil out of the gorge using a pack train of mules. He sold the oil to the makers of patent medicine in the United States and shipped at least 2000 gallons to Europe for use in liniments and other cure-alls. By 1820, Huling had given up the oil business because of the difficulty of transporting the oil to market and went back to drilling for salt in other places in the region. Yet, because some of the oil was actually sold, the Beaty Well, typically named for the landowner, qualifies as the first documented commercial oil well in the United States. Although there had been similar oil strikes at other drillings for salt, there is no documentation to show that any of the oil was sold from those earlier wells.

You can visit the site of the Beaty Well, with a little difficulty. From the Yamacraw Bridge crossing of the Big South Fork on KY92, on the west side of the river, turn south on KY1363. At 2.5 miles, turn left on a road that crosses Rock Creek on a concrete bridge; you'll see a sign for Bald Knob and Wilson Ridge. After the bridge, the road consists of gravel and broken pavement. Pass through the community of Beech Grove, dip through a cove, and head up the mountain. After ascending steeply, you'll reach Bald Knob and the Bald Knob Road to the left at 7.4 miles; turn left. At 1.6 miles down Bald Knob Road, you'll find parking for the Ledbetter Place Trailhead. The road beyond the trailhead has been improved to give access to a cemetery at its end, but it can still be muddy in places after a rain. From the trailhead, continue by walking down the road another 0.6 mile to a trail turnoff on the right; you could drive to this spot, but there's not much room for parking more than one car beside the road. Blazed with a red arrow, the trail, part of the Kentucky Trail, descends southeast along an old roadway that can get quite overgrown in summer. At 1.4 miles, the trail fords Oil Well Branch and then parallels the river where in about 500 feet the old well is off to your left between the trail and the river—just a pipe sticking out of the ground. A sign in the woods off the trail marks the spot. When the well was rediscovered after the turn of the century, the original rotting wooden casing was replaced with the pipe and a screw cap.

Oil and, in later years, gas became big business in the Big South Fork region. But the two largest extraction industries were timbering and coal mining. Cutting trees for lumber occurred on a small scale probably as far back as when the first communities took shape, and coal mining occurred at least as early as 1838.

Once these two industries began to expand, they contributed to a steady increase in the region's population. The last group of immigrants were the managers and workers needed to run the railroads, coal mines, and lumbering operations of a large industrial development that occurred between 1900 and 1930. The development was made possible by the completion in 1880 of the Southern Railway, which linked Cincinnati, Ohio, with Chattanooga. People and equipment could arrive by rail, and coal and lumber could be shipped out.

Lumber stacked to dry at Stearns Lumber Mill
(Courtesy of Stearns Museum)

The largest operation was the Stearns Coal and Lumber Company founded in 1902 by Justus S. Stearns, a Michigan industrialist. The coal and lumber companies were at first separate but later merged. Stearns, Kentucky, was founded as the headquarters of the company, which eventually commanded many thousands of acres of land in the Big South Fork region. The company's band sawmill for cutting lumber was located at Stearns.

In its peak year of 1929, the Stearns Company produced 1,000,000 tons of coal and 18,000,000 board feet of lumber. It employed 2000 miners and several hundred loggers, including many of the local people. To get this lumber and coal from the backwoods to the Southern Railroad line at Stearns, the company established its own Kentucky & Tennessee Railroad, which ran down into the Big South Fork gorge and then followed the river north to cross on a ballast-filled, concrete arch bridge at Yamacraw erected in 1907; the train then proceeded up Rock Creek.

A number of company towns were established along the K&T to support the industry—Worley, Barthell, and Yamacraw among them. Since there was not much level land in the valleys, and the rail line and the mining operations took up most of that, the towns stretched along the stream banks and up the mountainside on stilts.

The Stearns Company was relatively benevolent, establishing schools in the work camps, not requiring workers to live in company housing, and encouraging the workers to continue farming by being willing to hire part-time, leasing land to those who had none, and establishing a demonstration farm just outside of town. Health care in the camps was often better than in the surrounding rural areas.

While the Stearns Company strongly resisted unionization of their miners, the wages it paid were comparable to what the unions were asking and

Stearns band sawmill
(Courtesy of Stearns Museum)

the mines were some of the safest in the country. In addition, Stearns often led the way in mining technology; by 1914 the company mined with electric equipment. As a result, many miners were already satisfied working for the Stearns Company. But the unions tried to organize anyway. The company's resistance to unionization included intentionally burning the company's hotel in Stearns to rout union leaders who were occupying the building and who had killed a federal marshal trying to enforce a warrant. Because of the resistance of the company and their fellow miners, those who wanted to hold union meetings often gathered in the refuge of rock shelters, following in the tradition of Native American hunting parties, longhunters, and early settlers of the region.

K&T train on the bridge at Yamacraw
(Courtesy of Stearns Museum)

In the Tennessee region, the Tennessee Stave and Lumber Company and the New River Lumber Company were the largest operations. The Oneida & Western Railroad served to link Tennessee Stave's logging operations with the Southern Railway line in Oneida; the rail line crossed the Big South Fork on a 200-foot Whipple Truss bridge that was salvaged from another location and erected over the river in 1914 or 1915. Independent lumbering and mining operations also opened along the new railroad, which eventually ran as far west as Jamestown. Small communities and camps such as

O&W Depot in Oneida
(Courtesy of Audney Lloyd)

Toomey, Gernt, and Zenith grew up around the stops along the O&W where coal and lumber were loaded into the rail cars. The Tennessee Stave band mill stood on the rail line just west of Oneida at Verdun, named for Verdun, France, which withstood repeated German assaults in World War I. The New River Company had a mill at the community of New River and a larger mill farther east at Norma.

For a time, the region experienced an economic boom. But with the Depression of the 1930s that resulted in a lack of demand for coal and lumber, economic prospects declined. The downturn also resulted from the easily accessible timber and coal becoming exhausted and from conflicts between labor and management. The demands of World War II provided some reprieve, but the industries were never to fully recover. By 1948, the out-migration had begun. Stearns closed its Yamacraw mines in 1949 and the Worley mines in 1953. The O&W Railroad ceased operation in 1954.

K&T Engine #11 at Blue Heron
(Courtesy of Stearns Museum)

Stearns had opened its Blue Heron Mining operation in 1938 to bolster its operations. A number of mines were located along both sides of the river. Smaller in population than many of the older mining camps because of the use of state-of-the-art technology, Blue Heron operated until 1962, producing over 5 million tons of coal. The output was enough to keep mines operating but never reached expected levels. Stearns sold its last mining operations, which were outside the Big South Fork boundaries, in 1975.

The coal company towns, lumber mills, and rail lines gradually disappeared. Some coal mining continued, along with oil and gas exploration. But for the most part, the forest and river gorge were left in silence to heal.

Traces and Sites of Extractive Industries

Exploring some of the back roads in the BSFNRRA, you can occasionally still see oil pumping stations and tanks or pipes and a manifold emerging from a natural gas line. Both oil and gas production are still allowed within the park boundaries in the adjacent rim area, but not in the gorge area; operations are presently located mostly in the southern area of the park. There are around

300 oil and gas well sites within the national area. The Park Service monitors this use of the park to ensure sites and roads are properly constructed and reclaimed.

Second-growth timber now hides the effects of the lumbering operations that cut most of the forests of the Big South Fork. Driving some of the back roads in the southern part of the park or along the highways outside the park, you'll occasionally see pine monocultures that remain from more recent lumbering operations.

In contrast, you can still see many of the remains of the mining industry. You can visit the old Blue Heron Mining Community in the Kentucky portion of the park by either driving KY742 and Mine 18 Road down to the community or riding the Big South Fork Scenic Railway that follows the old K&T line from Stearns down to Blue Heron. Before reaching the mining community, the train crosses Roaring Paunch Creek on a trestle that was originally on the New York Central Railway at Lyon, New York; girders and steel support towers were salvaged and the bridge was erected here in 1937. If you're driving down to Blue Heron, you'll see the trestle to the right where the train tracks cross the road and you make a sharp left curve to enter the community.

Tram bridge at Blue Heron
(Courtesy of Stearns Museum)

Blue Heron is a reconstructed historic site. Originally all that remained was the tipple, a giant contraption for screening coal into different sizes that began operation in 1938; the vibrating screens and conveyors were driven by nineteen motors. The separated and picked-over coal dropped down chutes into railroad cars below to be hauled out of the river gorge. The rest of the community disappeared through dismantling and decay, but twelve of the old buildings and houses have been resurrected as "ghost" structures, roofs on pilings that give you an idea of what the community once looked like. You can walk the short Blue Heron Trail that takes you through the community. You'll find especially intriguing the recorded voices of the people who lived and worked in the community; within each of the structures, push a button to play the recordings; each has a different theme having to do with the way of life there.

Behind the old tipple lies one of the entrances to Mine 18, also called the "Blue Heron Mine." Blue Heron was the Stearns Company name for an intermediate grade of coal. You can also walk across the top of the tipple and then across the tram bridge that crosses the river, a total span of 975 feet. The coal company once hauled coal from mines along both sides of the river by tramcars pulled by electric motors. The bridge allowed the tramcars from the west side to cross the river and pass over the tipple where the drop-bottom cars released their loads.

The bridge now gives access to hiking trails that follow the old tram rail-beds on the west side of the river. Following the hiking trail north along the old tram road for about 0.3 mile, you'll see upright posts that remain from the line of utility poles that carried electricity along the tram track. South along the tram road you'll see discarded tramcars beside the trail on the left and coal littered along the path.

A section of trail, which turns left off this main trail at 0.2 mile, has been abandoned because of slides. A proposal calls for fixing the trail. When it reopens as part of the Catawba Overlook Loop, you'll be able to continue south following the old tramline bed past a gated mine opening.

Hiking any of the trails in the area, you'll likely see streams stained bright orange or yellow-brown. This is the result of acid mine drainage; when acid water flowing from a coal mine makes contact with the air, iron sulfate precipitates out. This precipitate, called "yellow boy," gives the stream its discoloration. The Park Service has an active project to address the yellow-boy problem.

Most mined areas in the park have been reclaimed. From the Devils Jump Overlook, you'll see a reclaimed spoils pile below. A field of debris was dumped there from a mine, but the area has been reclaimed with topsoil and perennial grasses and, at the upper end, a stand of pine trees.

Big South Fork Structures Eligible for the National Register of Historic Places

Historic American Building Survey

Charit Creek Lodge on Station Camp Creek
John Blevins Four-Crib Barn at Charit Creek Lodge
John Blevins Corncrib at Charit Creek Lodge
John Blevins Log Blacksmith Shop at Charit Creek Lodge
John B. Blevins Log House at Oscar Blevins Farm Site
John B. Blevins Corncrib at Oscar Blevins Farm Site
Lora Blevins Log House at Lora E. Blevins Farmstead
Lora Blevins Log Barn at Lora E. Blevins Farmstead
Lora Blevins Corncrib at Lora E. Blevins Farmstead
John Litton Log House at John Litton (General Slaven) Farm
John Litton English-Style Barn at John Litton (General Slaven) Farm

Historic American Engineering Resources

K&T Bridge over the Big South Fork at Yamacraw
K&T Trestle over Roaring Paunch Creek near Blue Heron
Blue Heron Tipple at the Blue Heron Mining Community
O&W Bridge over the Big South Fork south of Leatherwood Ford
Low-water bridge at Leatherwood Ford

Part II
Outdoors at the Big South Fork

Hiking

Hiking is the most popular activity in the park and the easiest in which to participate. Even if you come to the park for some other outdoor activity, you'll probably end up taking a stroll through the woods to see a natural arch or an overlook or just to stretch your legs.

There are about 200 miles of designated hiking trails in the BSFNRRA. The trails range from less than a mile to as much as 40 miles in length; most are suitable for day hikes. Many can be combined for long hikes and back-packing trips. Hikers may also use the horse trails, but you should give horses the right-of-way by quietly standing to the lower side of the trail and allowing them to pass. In addition, old roads in the park are interesting to explore.

If you ask or read about the difficulty of a trail, you'll usually be told that it is easy, moderate, or strenuous. The degree of difficulty is usually based on the ability of an average person, someone who occasionally hikes but for whom a long hike is not a frequent occurrence. So more experienced hikers may find what are described as moderate hikes quite easy and the strenuous hikes fairly moderate. Someone who rarely hikes will find the moderate and perhaps the easy trails strenuous.

A rating is usually based on a subjective judgment of the strenuousness of the trail—how much up and down there is, how difficult are the stream crossings, whether the footing on the trail is rocky or overgrown. As a result, while a 10-mile trail would be difficult for anyone not used to hiking, it might be called easy if it is relatively level, has no creek crossings, and is fairly easy walking. So if you are not accustomed to hiking, look not only at the degree of difficulty, but also at the distance you will walk (double that if the trail is one-way and so does not form a loop; you'll also have to walk back). You might also ask about any particular areas of caution that you will encounter on a trail, such as creek crossings, rocky footing, mud holes, and steep climbs and descents. When deciding whether you're up to hiking a particular trail, you'll need to take these cautions into consideration and be prepared.

Hiking Safety

Before setting out on a hike, make sure you have a map showing the trail you are taking and the surrounding area. Also, you'll need the basic shoes, clothing, rain gear, water, lunch, insect repellent, and first-aid kit described earlier in the section on what to bring when visiting the park. Just in case you get lost, you should also take along a compass, extra clothes, a knife, a flashlight, and a lighter or waterproof matches plus firestarter for building a fire. If you do get lost or need to make an injured person comfortable, you'll also be glad you brought along a plastic sheet or emergency blanket.

Trail maps are available through the visitor centers, where you can also purchase one of the hiking guides for detailed directions. You might secure a map and hiking guide prior to coming to the park so you can plan ahead. Read through the trail descriptions, plan your route, and study the trail connections while looking at a map of the entire park. The park rangers will be glad to give you additional information about a trail and the current conditions.

All the designated hiking trails in the Big South Fork are marked with a red arrowhead in a white blaze, with the exceptions of the John Muir Trail, which has a blue silhouette of Muir on a white blaze; the Sheltowee Trace, which has a white or sometimes blue turtle and white diamonds; the Yahoo Falls trails, which have yellow, green, and blue blazes; and occasionally a connector trail that has an arrowhead blaze of blue or gray. The blazes are usually spaced

John Litton Farm

close enough you will see one ahead whenever you begin to wonder if you have strayed from the trail. You might also look behind to see a blaze in the other direction to ensure you are still on the trail.

Once at the trailhead, you should be able to find your way by following the map and guidebook and reading the signs at most trail junctions. You are expected to assume responsibility for knowing where you are going and for not getting lost. Always let someone know where you are going and give them an expected return time so he or she can contact park authorities if you don't show up. To keep from getting lost, watch for trail signs and blazes, stay on the trails, and don't overestimate your ability. Hiking in plateau gorge country can be difficult because of the rugged terrain; inexperienced hikers often underestimate the difficulty and so also underestimate the time required to cover a trail. If, while hiking, you do not know where to go forward, but you remember the way you came, you might try backtracking until you reach a

location in which you know where you are, rather than continuing forward and becoming more confused. Do not leave the trail if you get lost; search teams will cover the trails first when looking for you.

To help preserve the area, do not cut across switchbacks; taking shortcuts that others then follow causes erosion. And resist the temptation to skirt muddy areas; walking around widens the trail and destroys vegetation.

It is best to hike with someone. Then if one of you falls or turns an ankle, someone will be there to care for the injured person. If the injured cannot make it back to the trailhead, make the person warm and comfortable, leave someone to tend the person if there is a third hiker in your party,

Split Bow Arch

pay attention to the exact location, and then hike out and contact the park rangers who will help in rescuing the injured person.

Stream crossings can be quite easy or quite difficult. Many crossings have sturdy bridges, but many others do not and you may have to ford. After a heavy rain, a stream can be swollen with rushing water and is often more hazardous than it appears. Do not attempt to cross such a stream unless you are sure you can make it. When the water level is down, you'll find that you can rockhop most streams, but this can also be hazardous if the rocks are wet; use caution and be prepared to slip. If you decide to wade across, wear shoes to protect your feet; some hikers carry along old tennis shoes or sandals to change into for stream crossings. Find a stick to use for balance. If you're carrying a pack, release the waist strap so you can slip out of the pack easily in case you fall. If you take a dunking and the water carries you away, float on your back with your feet downstream so you can ward off rocks until you have a chance to stop and get out of the water. Even when you are crossing a footbridge over a creek you should use caution; some can be wet and slippery or in winter covered with ice.

Be prepared for a change in the weather. On cooler days dress in layers so you can adjust your clothes as you warm up or cool down. And it rains frequently on the Plateau; so you should always have rain gear.

In addition, review all the precautions on snakes, insects, poison ivy, hypothermia, and emergencies mentioned earlier in the section on Planning a Visit. Don't be discouraged from walking the trails by all these warnings. The Big South Fork is well worth having to take a few precautions.

In addition to the trails listed below, three long trails (Kentucky Trail, John Muir Trail, and Sheltowee Trace) are discussed in the section on backpacking.

Hiking Trails of the Big South Fork

❶ The easy 3.6-mile **Oscar Blevins Farm Loop** leads from the Bandy Creek Trailhead to circle by the Blevins Farm; the trailhead is just down the road from the visitor center, on the left.

❷ The easy 2.3-mile **Bandy Creek Campground Loop** is a graveled path that begins at the Bandy Creek Trailhead and circles the campground, stables, and fields through an uplands forest, passing the Bandy Creek Visitor Center.

Hiking Trails of the Big South Fork

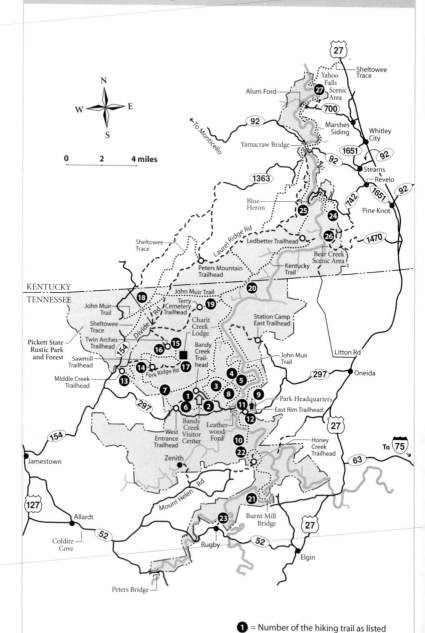

1 = Number of the hiking trail as listed

3 The moderate 5.9-mile **John Litton Farm Loop** passes a junction with the Fall Branch Trail and wanders through the Litton homeplace; start from the Bandy Creek Trailhead, or you can begin at the parking area next to the swimming pool.

4 The easy 1.9-mile **Fall Branch Trail** links the John Litton Farm Loop with the Grand Gap Loop.

5 The moderate 6.8-mile **Grand Gap Loop** skims the rim of the Big South Fork Gorge, offering some of the best views in the park; the trail can be accessed from the Bandy Creek Campground by the John Litton and Fall Branch Trails, or from Leatherwood Ford on the John Muir Trail to Angel Falls Overlook.

6 The easy 2.4-mile one-way **West Entrance Trail** connects the West Entrance Trailhead, just inside the park's west entrance on TN297, to the Oscar Blevins Farm Loop.

7 The strenuous 10.8-mile **Laurel Fork Trail** travels along Laurel Fork from the Slave Falls Loop in the Middle Creek Area to the John Muir Trail at Station Camp Creek, fording the creek numerous times; attempt only at low water. The trail can be accessed in the middle from the West Entrance Trailhead on a connector trail.

8 A moderate 3.0-mile one-way section of the John Muir Trail north from Leatherwood Ford on TN297 reaches the splendid **Angel Falls Overlook** of the Big South Fork.

9 The easy 2.0-mile one-way **Angel Falls Trail** north from Leatherwood Ford leads to a view of the rapids. Continuing north on this trail, you'll reach Station Camp Ford in another 6.1 miles; that trail section for horses along the east side of the river is called "River Trail East."

10 The moderate 3.0-mile one-way section of the John Muir Trail south from Leatherwood Ford arrives at the **O&W Railroad Bridge** over the Big South Fork; across the bridge the JMT turns south to reach the **Devils Den** rock shelter where, at this writing, the trail ends.

11 The moderate 3.6-mile **Leatherwood Ford Loop** from the East Rim Trailhead on the East Rim Overlook Road off TN297 leads to an overlook of Leatherwood Ford and descends to the river before looping back to the top of the plateau.

12 The easy 1.3-mile one-way **Sunset Overlook Trail**, also from the East Rim Trailhead, leads to another overlook of the river.

13 The moderate 3.5-mile **Middle Creek Nature Loop**, from the Middle Creek Trailhead on Divide Road on the west side of the park, passes by numerous rock shelters.

14 The easy 4.2-mile **Slave Falls Loop** from the Sawmill Trailhead on Fork Ridge Road in the Middle Creek area swings by Slave Falls and Indian Rockhouse. A 3.4-mile connector links the Slave Falls Loop with the Twin Arches/Charit Creek Loop along Mill Creek.

15 The easy 1.4-mile **Twin Arches Loop** from the Twin Arches Trailhead on Divide Road leads past the massive double arches.

16 The moderate 4.6-mile **Twin Arches/Charit Creek Loop** off the Twin Arches Loop circles by Twin Arches, Jakes Place, and Charit Creek Lodge.

17 The moderate 0.8-mile one-way **Charit Creek Trail** leads from the end of Fork Ridge Road down to Charit Creek Lodge.

18 The moderate 7.5-mile **Rock Creek Loop** that descends along an old railroad bed to Rock Creek begins at the Hattie Blevins Cemetery in the Middle Creek area; take Divide Road north 4.7 miles to Three Forks and turn left to reach the cemetery and trailhead.

19 An easy 1.1-mile walk along an old roadbed from the Terry Cemetery Trailhead leads to **Mauds Crack Overlook** for views of the No Business Creek Gorge. A difficult climb down through the crack in the bluff gives access to the John Muir Trail. The trailhead lies at the end of vehicle access on Terry Cemetery Road, which turns east off Divide Road at Three Forks just up the road from the left turn to the Rock Creek Loop.

20 The moderate 1.4-mile **Burkes Branch Trail** and the 0.8-mile **Dry Branch Trail** provide access to the John Muir Trail at No Business Creek. In the Middle Creek area, take Divide Road northeast 11.2 miles to the Peters Mountain Trailhead in Kentucky (the John Muir Trail crosses Divide Road at 6.7 miles). From Peters Mountain Trailhead, drive another 1.7 miles up Laurel Ridge Road (somewhat rough), park at the beginning of Laurel Hill Road on the right and walk down the trail 1.9 miles to the Burkes Branch Trail on the right (you can drive to this point, but Laurel Hill Road may not be suitable for passenger cars).

21 The moderate 3.6-mile **Burnt Mill Bridge Loop** from the Burnt Mill Bridge River Access follows the Clear Fork River.

22 The strenuous 5.2-mile **Honey Creek Loop** from the Honey Creek Trailhead provides one of the most interesting and intricate hikes in the park, with rock formations and waterfalls.

23 The moderate 2.0-mile **Gentlemen's Swimming Hole/Meeting of the Waters Loop** at Rugby leads down to the old swimming hole on the Clear Fork River; from TN52 in the historic community, turn north on the gravel road to Laurel Dale Cemetery.

24 The moderate 6.6-mile **Blue Heron Loop** out of the Blue Heron Mining Community passes through Cracks-in-the-Rock and circles to Devils Jump Rapids.

25 The moderate 3.6-mile one-way hike to **Catawba Overlook** and **Big Spring Falls** follows the old tram road on the west side of the river at Blue Heron; this route is part of the Kentucky Trail; at the Blue Heron Mining Community, walk across the tram bridge to the other side of the river and turn south to reach the overlook of river gorge in 1.6 miles; continue south another 2.0 miles to pass Dick Gap Falls and reach Big Spring Falls.

26 The easy 0.7-mile **Split Bow Arch Loop** in the Bear Creek Scenic Area passes through Split Bow Arch.

27 The moderate 0.8-mile **Topside Loop** and the moderate 0.2-mile **Cascade Loop** in the Yahoo Falls Scenic Area circle by Yahoo Falls and Roaring Rocks Cataract; there's also an easy 1.2-mile one-way **Yahoo Arch Trail** that leads into the surrounding national forest to a large natural arch.

Cross-Country Hiking

Hiking cross-country has its special rewards. This is true exploring, perhaps going where no one has set foot before, except maybe Native Americans who once hunted the region. You may discover an unknown arch or a never-before-seen waterfall.

You should not attempt to hike cross-country, even if this just means following unmarked old roads, unless you are an experienced hiker and navigator. If you intend to hike where there are no designated trails, you must have a compass and topographical maps and know how to use them together in a process called "orienteering" to determine your location. You will need to be especially careful while walking in areas of steep drop-offs, and of course, do not hike after dark when you cannot see where you're going. Take with you the minimum equipment required for backpacking in case you get lost and everything you need if you intend to spend the night outside.

Plan ahead and let a ranger know your intended route.

Backpacking

If you want to hike long distances or spend more time experiencing the Big South Fork, you'll probably want to backpack. Being out for several days at a time provides a rich experience and a good escape from the harried life. You can plan a backpacking route by combining the trails listed in the previous section on hiking or by taking one of the three long trails in the park.

The best backpacking trail is the John Muir Trail, named for the noted conservationist who in 1867 explored this Cumberland region before heading west to crusade for the establishment of national parks and found the Sierra Club. The easiest southern access for the John Muir Trail is at Leatherwood Ford. The trail then travels north for 40 miles passing through some of the most isolated backcountry in the park to end at Pickett State Rustic Park and Forest just west of the BSFNRRA. From Leatherwood Ford, the John Muir Trail also heads south on the east side of the river 2.3 miles to the O&W Bridge where it crosses and continues south to Devils Den rock shelter where it currently ends; plans call for an extension of the trail south to the Honey Creek area where another section of the trail heads south to Burnt Mill Bridge, adding another 7 miles. The John Muir Trail will eventually extend south all the way to the Peters Bridge River Access at the southern boundary of the park. That will add another 16 miles to the total length of the trail.

You'll find more remote backpacking along the 26-mile Kentucky Trail beginning at the Peters Mountain Trailhead. On the west side of the park, take Divide Road off TN154 east into the Middle Creek area. Stay with Divide Road, which becomes Peters Mountain Road when it crosses the state line, for 11 miles to the trailhead. The trail begins northeast on the Laurel Ridge Road but soon turns southeast off the road to cross the northern area of the park and pass through the Ledbetter Place Trailhead on Bald Knob Road. The trail continues north, past the tram bridge crossing the river to the Blue Heron Mining Community, and goes on to emerge on Wilson Ridge Road. It then follows the road north and eventually turns off to connect with the Sheltowee Trace. You can then follow the trace north to Yamacraw Bridge.

The Sheltowee Trace National Recreation Trail also provides for long-distance hiking. The trail is named for Daniel Boone, who was given the name "Sheltowee," meaning "Big Turtle," by the Shawnee, who were holding him captive at the time. This 257-mile trail passes north to south through Kentucky's Daniel Boone National Forest, entering the BSFNRRA at Big Creek on the northern end of the park. The easiest access for this trail section is at the Yahoo Falls Scenic Area. The trail then heads south along the Big South Fork through Alum Ford to cross to the west side at Yamacraw Bridge. The trace reenters Daniel Boone National Forest at Yamacraw and then parallels the northern boundary of the BSFNRRA southwest to eventually follow Rock Creek and cut through the northwest corner of the park and end at Pickett State Rustic Park and Forest at the same point as the John Muir Trail. From the Yahoo Falls Scenic Area to Pickett State Rustic Park and Forest is a distance of 40 miles.

For backpacking, you will of course need everything for surviving in the open overnight and for however many days you choose to be out. If you are inexperienced in backpacking, the park rangers or your local outfitters can give advice on the equipment needed. If it's your first time out, you should go with someone experienced in backpacking. Keep in mind all the precautions mentioned in the section on hiking safety.

At the minimum, you should have along a trail map that gives you an overall view of the park and the trail connections. But you'll probably want more detailed information than a trail map provides. Look at the topographical maps that cover the area you will be hiking. The most useful are the 1:24,000 quads (the 7.5 minute series). Topographical maps are available from your local map supplier or at the park visitor centers.

Plan ahead. Read through the trail descriptions in a hiking guide prior to going, plan your route, and study the trail connections while looking at an overall map of the park. Ask the rangers about the current conditions of the trails and about any problem areas, such as stream crossings without bridges or trails that have not been cleared of fallen trees. Use the normal precautions when crossing streams; be sure to release the hip belt of your backpack when fording so you can easily slip out of the pack if you fall in the water.

Backcountry registration is not required at this time, but you'll be wise to let a ranger know your plans. You can register at the Bandy Creek Visitor Center and the Kentucky Visitor Center. At least let a friend or member of your family know where you intend to be so they can contact the park staff if you get into trouble and do not return when expected.

It is best to backpack with someone. Then if one of you is injured, the other person will be there to attend to the injuries and to go for help.

You may camp virtually anywhere in the backcountry, but set up at least 25 feet from trails, gravel and dirt roads, rock shelters, the gorge rim, and major geologic and historic features and at least 100 feet from streams and the center line of paved roads, 200 feet from parking lots and other developed areas and then only if you cannot be seen, and 200 feet from cemeteries and gravesites.

If you are in a high use area, camp at an existing site rather than damage vegetation at a new site. In more remote areas, pick the site where you will cause the least damage. Near streams, and especially near the river, set up camp on a high area to avoid rising flood waters from rain upstream. Some areas that receive overuse may be temporarily closed to camping. At the established campgrounds, camping is permitted only in designated sites.

Plan to camp in the vicinity of the larger streams to be guaranteed a source of water; streams are noted on the topographic and trail maps. You can also get water from streams while you are hiking during the day; carry water with you in case no water is available when you need to stop for the night. Purify all water in the backcountry.

When camping, use only down and dead timber for campfires; build your fires on cleared ground and be sure to douse your fire with water and then make sure the coals are cold before leaving. Scatter the ashes to hide the site unless it has a frequently used fire ring. You may gather nuts and berries in reasonable quantities for your personal use, but make sure you know what you're eating; some berries and nuts are toxic.

At night, hang your food on a rope between two trees to keep it away from animals. Bury your waste at least six inches deep and 100 feet away from trails, water sources, and campsites. Do not bury sanitary napkins or tampons; instead, add them to your trash bag and carry them out. Do not wash dishes in a stream; take water from the streams to do your washing and let the waste water drain onto the ground. Use the same procedure if you plan on bathing with soap instead of just splashing around in the water.

When breaking camp, take down any ropes or branches you have used in making camp. Pack out all trash and litter. And take a last look to ensure you have left no trace of having been there.

Horseback Riding

The BSFNRRA is one of the best places in the Southeast for horseback riding. The park has 200 miles of trails specifically designed for horses. The horse trails have a yellow or orange silhouette of a horse's head on a white blaze. Horses may not use the designated hiking or biking trails or paved roads. And you may not ride cross-country. But in addition to the horse trails there are many miles of unmarked roads that you may explore; if a road is overgrown with trees and brush or if it is blazed for hiking or mountain biking, it is not open to horse traffic.

You can get a trail map at the visitor centers that shows both hiking and horse trails. You should take along the topographic maps that cover the area of your ride, also available at the visitor centers; many of the horse trails appear on the topos as old roads.

The Bandy Creek area can be your base of operations since many horse trails lead out from this area. At the Bandy Creek Stables, a concession within the park, you can rent a stall for your horse while you stay in the campground. Charit Creek Lodge also has stables for keeping horses overnight while riders stay at the lodge.

You may also rent horses at the Bandy Creek Stables for guided horseback rides of an hour or more or overnight trips of two or three days from April to mid-November, or for long trips in winter by prior arrangement. The minimum age for a rider is six years old; riders should weigh no more than 250 pounds. Overnights are spent at a backcountry camp or at Charit Creek Lodge; bring your own sleeping bag and personal items. You must make reservations. Don't forget to wear long pants. Bandy Creek Stables also offers wagon rides; contact the stables for details.

At this writing, two commercial operators located outside the park also offer horseback day rides and overnight pack trips in the park: Southeast Pack Trips and Tally Ho Stables. Check with the park visitor centers for any other stables that might be commercial operators at the time you visit the park.

In addition to the Bandy Creek complex, new equestrian camps can serve as the base from which to ride. An equestrian camp at Station Camp East has camping spaces with water and electricity, hitching posts, and a central bathhouse. A similar equestrian camp is located at the Bear Creek Scenic Area. These are fee campgrounds, as are the two other established campgrounds in the park. For reservations, contact the concessionaire that operates the camps, Big South Fork Horse Camps. (See Appendix A for telephone numbers and addresses.)

Rules for Riding

When you arrive at the park, you must have in your possession proof of a negative Coggins test for swamp fever (EIA) for your horse.

Plan your route ahead of time and study the trail connections with a topographical map. Ask the rangers about the current conditions of the trails and about any problem areas, such as stream crossings, river fords, and rock ledges that may be difficult to negotiate. You should let the rangers know where you are going, especially if you are exploring old roads; at least let a friend or member of your family know where you intend to be so they can contact the park staff if you get into trouble and do not return when expected. It is best to ride with someone. Then if one of you is injured, the other person will be there to attend to the injuries and to go for help.

Getting ready for the trail

Check the trail and topographic maps for creek crossings where horses can get water. Ask the rangers about recent weather; if there has been no rain recently, some of the creeks may be dry, and you can ask for recommendations of trails where water will be available. If there has been recent rain, the creeks will be running and puddles along the trail will sometimes provide suitable water. When watering at a creek, choose a rocky area along the stream to minimize bank erosion.

Although horses have the right-of-way on horse trails, be aware that hikers and bicycle riders are also allowed to use the trails. A horse can be quite intimidating to someone on the ground; so be courteous when encountering hikers and bicycle riders, and allow them time to step aside before riding by, at a walk.

Remember that a comfortable horse, correctly shod and properly packed, stands quieter and causes less trail wear. You can also minimize trail wear by keeping the horses in your group in single file and so avoid the creation of multiple trails. To avoid widening the trail, don't let your horse unnecessarily skirt shallow puddles and minor obstacles and do not take shortcuts across switchbacks. Let the park rangers know of down trees you encounter so they can be removed before trails are created going around the obstructions. When taking a rest stop, cross-tie your horse off the trail to minimize trail wear. Because of the possible presence of endangered plant species, try not to let your horse graze.

Horseback riding at the Big South Fork

Hitching rails are often provided at locations where you must walk to geologic or historic sites.

When taking rest stops or camping in the backcountry, horses should be tied on picket lines away from trees, buildings, and at least 100 feet from water sources. You should acquaint your horse with picket ropes, hitch lines, and hobbles prior to your trip so you and the horse will not have trouble in the backcountry. As a courtesy to fellow campers, horses should not be kept in camp, but rather tied some distance away.

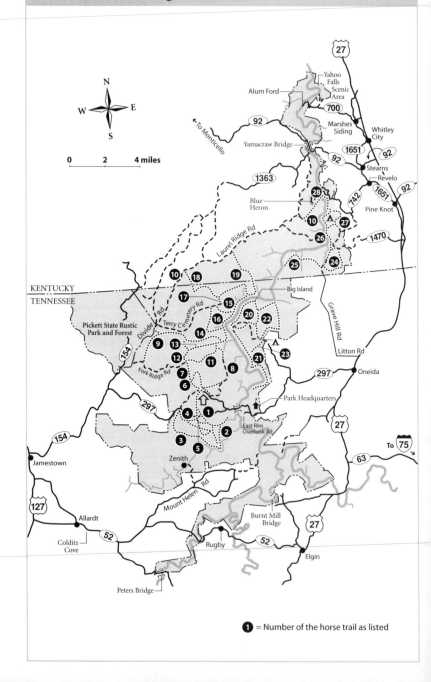

Horse Trails of the Big South Fork

27

Yahoo Falls Scenic Area

Alum Ford

700

Marshes Siding

Whitley City

92

To Monticello

N
W   E
S

0   2   4 miles

Yamacraw Bridge

1651

92

Stearns

Revelo

1363

742

1651

92

Blue Heron

28

Pine Knot

10

27

1470

26

24

25

Laurel Ridge Rd

Grave Hill Rd

KENTUCKY
TENNESSEE

10   18   19

Big Island

17

15

Pickett State Rustic Park and Forest

Terry Cemetery Rd

16   20   22

Divide Rd

154

9   13   14

21   23

Litton Rd

Fork Ridge Rd

12

11   8

297

Oneida

7

6

297

4   1

East Rim Overlook Rd

Park Headquarters

2

154

3   5

27

63

To 75

Jamestown

Zenith

127

Allardt

52

Mount Helen Rd

Burnt Mill Bridge

27

Colditz Cove

Rugby

52

Elgin

Peters Bridge

1 = Number of the horse trail as listed

You may camp virtually anywhere in the backcountry away from roads and geologic and historic sites. Registration is not required at this time, but it's a good idea to let the rangers know where you intend to camp. When selecting a campsite, look for one that can withstand the impact of horses and does not have to be cleared of vegetation. Grazing is by permit only. If horses are left to graze, move the picket line frequently to prevent overgrazing. Grass for grazing in the backcountry is limited anyway, so you'll need to bring feed along. When breaking camp, always remove any hitching ropes or picket lines you've tied to trees, scatter your horse's manure, and pack out all trash.

Each spring, the Big South Fork Competitive Ride takes place, sanctioned by the North American Trail Ride Conference and sponsored by the Knoxville Arabian Horse Club. Riders are judged on handling and conditioning of the horse. Contact NATRC for details.

Horse Trails of the Big South Fork

❶ The 17.5-mile **North White Oak Loop** starts at the Bandy Creek Equestrian Trailhead along the South Bandy Creek Trail, then goes south to cross TN297 to the loop part of the ride; a soft and sandy tread, level to gentle hills. The trail takes you by a 1.5-mile side trail to an overlook of Leatherwood Ford and a 1.6-mile side trail to an overlook of North White Oak Creek. To get to the Bandy Creek Trailhead, continue on the Bandy Creek Road past the visitor center and turn left just before the pavement ends; you'll pass a parking area and restrooms for the hiking trailhead and continue on to the equestrian trailhead; you'll see a corral there, available for day use only.

❷ The **Coyle Branch Trail** off the North White Oak Loop leads south along the old Coyle Branch Road toward North White Oak Creek and descends to the old O&W Railroad bed in 5.1 miles from the Bandy Creek Equestrian Trailhead; be aware the descent is rough and rocky. You can make a loop ride by then turning west on the O&W Railbed to the Gernt Trail and returning to the North White Oak Loop for a total of 17 miles roundtrip from the Bandy Creek Equestrian Trailhead.

❸ The 3.3-mile one-way **Gernt Trail** begins at the Cumberland Valley Trailhead on a side road next to the Hitching Post Grocery that is one mile outside the west park boundary on TN297. The trail follows the old Gernt Road, heading south toward North White Oak Creek and descending to the O&W Railbed; a difficult descent, rocky and rough.

4 The 2.4-mile one-way **Groom Branch Trail** heads east from the Cumberland Valley Trailhead, crossing Groom Branch and connecting with the North White Oak Loop; this trail serves to connect the Gernt Trail with the Loop. A Cumberland Valley Loop incorporates the Groom Branch Trail, North White Oak Loop, Coyle Branch Trail, and Gernt Trail for a 13.5-mile ride from the Cumberland Valley Trailhead.

5 The 2.3-mile one-way **Gar Blevins Trail** passes through the heart of the North White Oak Loop and connects with the North White Oak Overlook Trail to reach the overlook in another 1.6 miles; the Gar Blevins Trail begins on the south side of TN297 2.9 miles west of the road to the Bandy Creek Visitor Center.

6 The 8.2-mile **Jacks Ridge Loop** begins at the Bandy Creek Equestrian Trailhead and follows the North Bandy Creek Trail north and the Katie Trail west to the Jacks Ridge Road for a loop through plateau forest.

7 The 2.0-mile one-way **Black House Branch Trail** connects the Jacks Ridge Loop with the Middle Creek area, emerging on Fork Ridge Road near the Charit Creek Lodge in 4.2 miles from the Bandy Creek Equestrian Trailhead.

8 The **Duncan Hollow Trail**, accessed from the Bandy Creek Equestrian Trailhead by the North Bandy Creek and the Katie Trails, leads 6.0 miles along the old Duncan Hollow Road; smooth tread, often muddy in wet weather; the trail fords Laurel Fork and Station Camp Creek near the end to connect with the Station Camp Creek Trail. Beginning at the Bandy Creek Campground, the Duncan Hollow Road is open to vehicles for the first 4.2 miles.

9 **Gobblers Knob Trail** leads north from the Middle Creek Equestrian Trailhead, which is on Fork Ridge Road off Divide Road, 1.9 miles from TN154. This is a wide graveled path that is also used for wagon rides. The trail ends at the Gobblers Knob Trailhead on Terry Cemetery Road in 6.4 miles.

10 The **Long Trail** combines several trails for a long ride. From the Middle Creek Equestrian Trailhead, ride north on the Gobblers Knob Trail to connect with Divide Road (hard packed and gravel) at Terry Cemetery Road. Stay northeast on Divide Road to the Kentucky/Tennessee State

Line where it becomes the Peters Mountain Road and continue on to the Peters Mountain Trailhead, where you can also begin rides. The trail then continues along Laurel Ridge Road (hard packed and gravel), past the Laurel Hill Trail to the right and Bald Knob Road also to the right, and then beyond to turn down Waters Cemetery Road. Soon after, turn north to head to Blue Heron for a total of 25.8 miles. You must descend a steep rocky roadbed and ford the river to get across to Blue Heron at the river access ramp where you can connect with the Laurel Branch Trail that heads upstream along the river. The complex of trails considered the Long Trail also includes a loop up Terry Cemetery Road and along the Hatfield Ridge Trail and the Charit Creek Horse Trail to Fork Ridge Road and back to the Middle Creek Equestrian Trailhead. Another loop turns down the Laurel Hill Trail to Miller Branch Trail and then south on the River Trail West and up the Station Camp Creek Trail to Charit Creek Lodge and back to the Middle Creek Equestrian Trailhead.

11 The **Fork Ridge Trail** follows an old section of the Fork Ridge Road east from the improved section of Fork Ridge Road near the Charit Creek Horse Trail 3.5 miles to a junction with the Duncan Hollow Trail at Laurel Fork; good tread until the roadbed becomes a steep, rocky trail with ledges and fallen trees; this section is closed at this writing but is designated to be rerouted. Begin the ride at the Charit Creek Equestrian Trailhead at 4.5 miles along Fork Ridge Road from Divide Road in the Middle Creek area.

12 The 1.5-mile **Charit Creek Lodge Trail** leads down to Charit Creek Lodge from the end of vehicle access on Fork Ridge Road with fords of Station Camp and Charit Creeks. You can reach the end of the road from the Bandy Creek Equestrian Trailhead along the Jacks Ridge Loop and the Black House Branch Trail 4.2 miles to the Fork Ridge Road. Or start at the Charit Creek Equestrian Trailhead, 4.5 miles along Fork Ridge Road. At Charit Creek Lodge you can spend the night; reservations are necessary.

13 The **Station Camp Creek Trail** leads from Charit Creek Lodge 3.2 miles east to a junction with the Duncan Hollow Trail and, 0.9 mile beyond, to the Station Camp Crossing of the river; smooth and sandy tread with little elevation but several fords of Station Camp Creek. At the river you can ford to connect with the Big Island Loop; make the river crossing to the east side only at low water (you'll need to skirt a section of big rocks instead of making the crossing straight across).

(14) The 9.9-mile **Hatfield Ridge Loop** from Charit Creek Lodge follows the Station Camp Creek Trail east but, before reaching the river, turns north up Hatfield Ridge to circle back to the lodge with views and a side trail to the Charit Creek Overlook along the way; good tread; steep grades ascending and descending the ridge.

(15) The 4.4-mile one-way **River Trail West** travels along the west side of the Big South Fork from the Station Camp Crossing to the Big Island Crossing, linking the Station Camp Creek Trail with the No Business Trail; you can also ford the river at either crossing to access the Big Island Loop.

(16) The **Terry Cemetery Loop** covers 6.1 miles from Terry Cemetery Road to the river and back. At 4.9 miles up Divide Road from TN154, turn east on Terry Cemetery Road and drive to the Gobblers Knob Trailhead in another 1.4 miles. Ride from the Gobblers Knob Trailhead 3.6 miles past the Parch Corn Creek Road to the Watson Cemetery Road at the beginning of the Terry Cemetery Loop. Head down the old Watson Cemetery Road to the river and then south along the river to Parch Corn Creek Road and then up the road past the site of the John Litton Cabin and back to Terry Cemetery Road.

(17) The 0.7-mile one-way **Longfield Branch Trail** and the 3.1-mile one-way **No Business Trail** provide access from the Terry Cemetery Trailhead to the river ford at Big Island Crossing. Drive to the end of the Terry Cemetery Road to the Terry Cemetery Trailhead and take the Longfield Branch Trail down to a ford of No Business Creek. On the other side, turn right on the No Business Trail to follow the creek downstream past a junction with the Stoopin' Oak Road and Miller Branch Trail to the Big Island Crossing. At the river, you can turn south to cross No Business Creek and continue on the River Trail West or ford the river to access the Big Island Loop.

(18) The 3.8-mile **Stoopin' Oak Road** provides additional access to No Business Creek. At 10.1 miles along Divide Road from TN154, Stoopin' Oak Road turns to the east and descends into the No Business Gorge to connect with the No Business Trail.

(19) The 2.4-mile one-way **Laurel Hill Trail** and the 2.1-mile one-way **Miller Branch Trail** provide access from the Peters Mountain Trailhead to No Business Creek. Divide Road from Tennessee crosses the state line into Kentucky and becomes the Peters Mountain Road that leads to the

Peters Mountain Trailhead at 11.2 miles from TN154. From the trailhead, ride up Laurel Ridge Road 1.7 miles and turn right on the Laurel Hill Trail, which follows the old gravel Laurel Hill Road. Where vehicle access ends, the Laurel Hill Trail ends and the Miller Branch Trail continues by descending into the river gorge to a junction with the No Business Trail; the Big Island Crossing is 0.5 mile to the east.

20 The 11-mile **Big Island Loop** begins on the east side of the river at the Station Camp Crossing or can be reached by a connecting trail from the Station Camp East Trailhead or the Station Camp Equestrian Camp on Station Camp Road; tread is gravel but muddy in places. You'll pass a side trail to the Dome Rockhouse, with a hitching rail in the shade. At Big Island, you can ford the river to connect with the River Trail West, but it's muddy on both sides of the river; ford only at low water. On the east side of the river about a mile south of Big Island stands the Burke Cabin, a hunting and fishing cabin built in the 1970s that has been restored by volunteers and may be used for overnight stays. At the Station Camp Crossing, you can ford the river at low water to access the lower end of the River Trail West and the Station Camp Creek Trail.

21 At Station Camp Crossing, on the east side of the river, you can also head south along the **River Trail East** for 6.1 miles for access to Angel Falls; you must hitch your horse and walk the last bit to get to the view of the rapids.

22 The 14.8-mile **Pilot/Wines Loop** begins at the Station Camp East Trailhead and the adjacent horse camp at 4.5 miles along the Station Camp Road. The trail passes Pilot Rock, a massive block of sandstone sitting at the gorge rim, then dips to the river before climbing back to the trailhead.

23 A 0.9-mile one-way **Station Camp East Overlook Trail** leads west from the Station Camp East Trailhead to an overlook of the Big South Fork Gorge.

24 A 10.7-mile **Cotton Patch Loop** starts at the Slavens Branch Trailhead, dips several times to cross streams making up Bear Creek, and returns, fording Bear Creek near its confluence with the Big South Fork. To get to the Slavens Branch Trailhead, turn west off US27 on Litton Road 0.9 mile north of the junction of US27 and TN297 in Oneida. In 0.1 mile bear left on Grave Hill Road, and at 0.5 mile keep right to stay on Grave Hill Road. At 2.1 miles keep left and you'll arrive at Foster Crossroads in 7.4 miles.

(Or if you're coming from the park on TN297, at 3.8 miles east of the right turn off TN297 at the Terry and Terry Store, turn north on Williams Creek Road. Then at 4.5 miles turn right on the road that leads past the Pine Creek Baptist Church. You'll connect with the Grave Hill Road at 5.9 miles. Continue left on Grave Hill another 5 miles to Foster Crossroads.) At the Foster Cross Road Baptist Church, take the far right gravel road 1.0 mile down to cross the state line into Kentucky and also the boundary of the park onto Little Bill Slaven Road. You'll reach the trailhead on the right at 2.8 miles.

25 The 3.4-mile **Cub Branch Trail** begins on Huling Branch Road, 0.6 mile back down Little Bill Slaven Road from the Slavens Branch Trailhead. The trail descends to a crossing of Huling Branch and ascends from the creek to a junction with Cliff Terry Road, which leads back to Foster Crossroads. Plans call for the trail to eventually lead south to a junction with the Pilot/Wines Loop out of the Station Camp East Trailhead.

26 The 6.1-mile **Bear Creek Loop** starts at the Bear Creek Equestrian Trailhead in the Bear Creek Scenic Area. The trail drops to the river and heads north to circle by the Bear Creek Equestrian Camp and return to the trailhead, linking with the Cotton Patch Loop along the way.

27 From the Bear Creek Equestrian Camp, the 5.6-mile **Lee Hollow Loop** circles north, connecting with the Laurel Branch Trail and providing access to Blue Heron, before circling back to the camp.

28 The 1.9-mile one-way **Laurel Branch Trail** provides access from Blue Heron to the Lee Hollow Loop while traveling upstream along the Big South Fork.

Camping

There are two general fee campgrounds in the park. The campsites are first-come, first-served. Use only down and dead timber for campfires. Do not use chainsaws to cut firewood.

The large Bandy Creek Campground with 190 campsites is open year-round. It's located in the Tennessee portion of the park near the Bandy Creek Visitor Center north of TN297 on the west side of the river. The facilities include sites with electric and water hookups, tent campsites, and universally accessible sites. The campground has playgrounds, a swimming pool, a sand volleyball court, and restroom/shower houses. Two group camps can be reserved by contacting the Ranger Office at the park headquarters; there are no electrical hookups in the group camps. Reservations for the Bandy Creek Campground may be made by calling the campground or on the Internet.

The smaller Blue Heron Campground in the Kentucky portion of the park is open April through November. It has forty-five sites for tent camping or RVs up to 35 feet; sites have water and electric hookups. The campground is north of the Mine 18 Road on the way to the Blue Heron Mining Community on the east side of the river. The campground has universally accessible sites, a play structure, and a restroom/shower house.

Camping at the Big South Fork

In addition to these, there are two new equestrian camps, each with camp-sites, bathhouse, and hitching posts. The camps are at Station Camp East and the Bear Creek Scenic Area. These are also fee campgrounds. Although these camps are designed for camping with horses, people without horses may also stay in available spaces if they are willing to camp with horses nearby. Contact the Big South Fork Horse Camps concessionaire for reservations. Refer to information for the horse camps listed in Appendix A.

Alum Ford at the end of KY700 past the Yahoo Falls Scenic Area has primitive camping with seven sites and pit toilets; no water or electricity and no fee.

You may camp virtually anywhere in the backcountry, but set up at least 25 feet from trails, gravel and dirt roads, rock shelters, the gorge rim, and major geologic and historic features, at least 100 feet from streams and the center line of paved roads, 200 feet from parking lots, trailheads, and other developed areas, but only if you will not be visible, and 200 feet from cemeteries and gravesites. If you intend to camp near the river, set up on a high area, because the river can rise rapidly from rain upstream, sometimes many feet in just a few hours.

You will occasionally find specified "no camping" areas, usually designated because an area has become overused. At the established campgrounds, camping is permitted only at designated sites, except by a special use permit.

Registration for back-country camping is not required at this time, but it is a good idea to tell someone where you intend to spend the night.

Camping at the Bandy Creek Campground

Backcountry Lodging

The only lodging within the park is at Charit Creek Lodge in the backcountry, accessible only by hiking and horse trails. Reservations are needed for this concessionaire facility; the lodge will take people who just walk in if there are rooms available, but don't count on it.

You'll have a special experience at Charit Creek Lodge, staying in the backcountry yet having your basic needs taken care of. The lodge rests in a hollow at the confluence of Charit and Station Camp Creeks. The main lodge building incorporates old log cabins, and the two bunkhouses are constructed

Charit Creek Lodge

from historic log cabins. Hiking and horse trails lead out from the lodge. Charit Creek can also be a base from which to do mountain biking.

At present, the lodge has two bunk rooms and two bunkhouse cabins that each sleep twelve people. If your group has as many as six people, you can get a room or bunkhouse to yourselves; otherwise, you will share space with other guests if more than four groups are registered. The lodge has long-range plans to build a few single cabins that can be rented by smaller groups, families, or individuals.

There is no electricity at Charit Creek. The rooms and cabins are heated by woodstoves in winter. At night you'll use kerosene lanterns. You'll wash in a solar-powered bathhouse with propane backup. Bed linens are provided, but you must bring your own towel and washcloth.

Breakfast and dinner are included in the lodging fee. Lunch can also be had by reservation for lodge guests and anyone else who plans on passing through. Up to twelve people at a time may stay at the lodge as hostel guests at a lower rate; bring your own bedroll and no meals are provided, but you do have use of the kitchen.

Stables with hay are available for lodge guests to board horses overnight. You may also leave a horse out to pasture. There is a fee for both.

The lodge is open year-round, except Christmas and Christmas Eve. Only hostel accommodations are available on Thanksgiving day.

The shortest routes to Charit Creek Lodge lead from the parking area at the end of Fork Ridge Road in the Middle Creek area. Horseback riders and mountain bikers can descend the steep road past the gate 1.5 miles to the lodge, while hikers can take the more scenic Charit Creek Trail 0.8 mile one-way. For longer and more scenic routes, horseback riders and mountain bikers can take the horse trails north from Bandy Creek, and hikers can walk the 0.7-mile Twin Arches Loop Trail to Twin Arches and connect with the Twin Arches/Charit Creek Loop where it's 1.1 miles left or 3.5 miles right along the loop to the lodge.

Paddling

The Big South Fork is rapidly becoming known as one of the major whitewater rivers of the Southeast. About 86 miles of the river and its tributaries flow through the national river and recreation area. Most of the river miles can be paddled either by canoe, kayak, or raft.

This is a free-flowing river for most of its length, and so paddling is seasonal. There are some sections at low water that are suitable for lazy tubing, and other sections with high water at times that should not be attempted by canoe or raft regardless of a paddler's experience. Between these extremes, the river offers a fun experience ranging from placid sections for beginners to whitewater with Class III and IV rapids and more for the advanced.

If you want to be out more than a day, you may camp next to the river on overnight trips. But always camp high above the river, which has been known to rise many feet overnight from rain upstream.

Kayaking the river system
(Courtesy of the NPS)

Motorized boats are permitted only on the section of main channel from the Blue Heron area north; they may operate from 0.1 mile below Devils Jump Rapids. This section constitutes the upper reaches of Lake Cumberland created by the Wolf Creek Dam far downstream on the Cumberland River.

If you have little experience with paddling whitewater, you should contact one of the local outfitters for a guided trip. At this writing, Sheltowee Trace Outfitters provides guided raft trips plus canoe rental and shuttle service. Contact the park visitor centers for any new outfitters that may now also provide guided trips in the area.

If you are experienced or going with friends who are experienced and intend to paddle the river on your own, you must bring your own equipment, study a description of the river in published river guides, arrange for a shuttle to get back to your vehicle, and use commonly recommended safety practices.

Safety Practices

- Plan ahead and let a park ranger know what you are doing.

- Do not attempt a part of the river for which you are not prepared by experience.

- Always wear an approved life jacket and helmet.

- Never boat alone; there should be two other boats in your party to assist if one boat has an accident.

- Notice weather conditions and dress appropriately; wool clothing or a wet suit may be necessary if the weather is cool. Be aware of the dangers of hypothermia, and be prepared to take planned action if one of your group shows symptoms.

- Scout all major rapids and set up throw ropes before attempting the run. Portage waterfalls, high rapids, and flow-through hazards.

- If your boat capsizes, hold on while getting upstream of the craft. Orient on your back with your feet downstream, toes pointed. Release the boat only if necessary, but stay upstream of the boat so you do not get pinned against a boulder. If you see that you are about to go over a drop or ledge, ball up to keep arms and legs from getting caught in crevices; once you're out of the rapid, resume the position with toes pointed downstream. Never try to stand up in fast water. When you reach a placid section of the river, then you can retrieve your boat and/or get out of the water.

- Carry along dry clothing and a first-aid kit in a secured waterproof container. You should also have in your craft a spare paddle, a bailer, extra flotation if in a canoe, and a throw line.

- On the narrower streams, watch for log jams that you may have to portage around.

River at low water below Leatherwood Ford

Before setting off on a river trip, determine if the river flow is within the recommended minimums and maximums. At the Leatherwood Ford gazebo, you'll find an LED readout that gives the stage (or depth) in feet at Leatherwood Ford. This can also be determined by three staff gages. The lower staff is on the second pier of the old wooden bridge; the middle staff stands to the left where you turn left down the portage steps just before the bridge; the third stands in the trees to the left as you walk down toward the bridge from the gazebo. Once you know the stage in feet, then use the conversion chart posted below the readout in the gazebo to convert feet to water flow in cubic feet per second (cfs); on the chart, the y-axis is feet and the x-axis is tenths of feet. See chart, "Recommended Minimum and Maximum Flow."

Flood stage at Leatherwood Ford

Bridge support at Worley

In addition, the U.S. Geological Survey has flow information on the Big South Fork at an Internet site (see Appendix A); click on Tennessee or Kentucky and go to the Cumberland River Basin. If you do not have access to a computer, you can call the Bandy Creek Visitor Center for the latest flow readings, given in cubic feet per second, and the stage, in feet. You can then use the chart in this book to compare the flow rate to the recommended minimums and maximums for the river or tributary sections you intend to paddle. The maximum you can handle is, of course, subjective and should be based on the skill of your group's least-experienced member. Also keep in mind the river can change in the time it takes you to get to the river and during the day while you're on the river, so pay attention to current weather conditions; a storm upstream can cause the river flow to increase.

In case of emergencies, telephones are located at Leatherwood Ford and Blue Heron. In addition to designated river access points, there are footpaths for walkout at several places. In the gorge section, you'll find a road at the confluence of the New and Clear Fork Rivers on the right that leads up to the Scott County Airport, a trail at Honey Creek on the left that leads up to the overlook road, and a trail at Pine Creek that connects with the O&W Railbed. From Leatherwood Ford to the Station Camp river ford, a trail parallels the river on the right that allows you to get back to Leatherwood Ford to the south or hike to Station Camp Crossing to the north. At Station Camp Crossing, you can walk up the Station Camp Road on the right, or follow a horse trail on the left side of the river to Charit Creek Lodge. Trails parallel both sides of the river from Station Camp Ford to Big Island; about a mile south of Big Island on the east side of the river, you can spend the night at the Burke Cabin up the slope that's also used by horse riders. Farther north, you can walk out at Williams Creek and Bear Creek, both on the right, and at Blue Heron.

River Access

In addition to the river access described in the accompanying chart, the Bear Creek Gage Road down from the Bear Creek Scenic Area can be used as river access if you want to carry a canoe or raft a steep half mile down from the gate. You'll find parking at the Bear Creek Equestrian Trailhead 0.3 mile south of the parking for the Bear Creek Overlook.

You can also walk the 0.4-mile trail down to the confluence to put in at that location. At 2.5 miles south of Oneida on US27 turn west on Niggs Creek Road toward the airport. Cross a bridge over the Norfolk-Southern Rail Line and immediately turn left on Helenwood Detour Road. At 3.5 miles turn right on Airport Road, and then at 4.7 miles stay straight onto a graveled road as the paved road curves to the right. The gravel road passes behind the Scott County Memorial Airport. At 7.5 miles keep left at a fork. You'll cross the boundary into the park at 7.9 miles, pass the Dewey-Phillips Family Cemetery on the right at 8.7 miles, and reach the end of the road at a turnaround and parking at 8.8 miles. Walk the gated road to the right, which descends into the river gorge. The road curves right at 0.4 mile and runs down to the rocky shore at 0.5 mile. You'll see the confluence of the two rivers to the left.

Access Points from South to North, Moving Downstream

1 The **Peters Bridge River Access** at the southern-most boundary of the BSFNRRA provides access to the Clear Fork River, one of the two primary tributary streams that create the Big South Fork. Take TN52 west from Rugby town center 9.5 miles to a left turn on the Peters Ford Road beside the Pleasant View Church of the Nazarene; you'll see a sign for the river access. The river bridge is then 4.5 miles along the road.

2 The **Rugby River Access** just 2.5 miles west of Rugby town center on TN52 provides additional access to the Clear Fork River. West of the town center, cross the high bridge over the Clear Fork and turn left down into the river gorge on the old route of TN52 to reach the Clear Fork.

3 **White Oak Creek Access** 0.9 mile east of Rugby on TN52 gives access to a primary tributary of the Clear Fork River. There is no sign there. On the west side of the bridge over White Oak Creek make a sharp turn on the north side of the highway down toward the old bridge you'll see below. Then follow a faint footpath that leads under the highway bridge to the water's edge.

Access to the Big South Fork River System

N
W — E
S

0   2   4 miles

To Monticello

27

14

Alum Ford

13

700

Marshes Siding

Whitley City

92

Yamacraw Bridge

12

92

1651

92

11

1363

Stearns
Revelo

Blue Heron

10

742

1651

92

Pine Knot

1470

Bear Creek Scenic Area

KENTUCKY
TENNESSEE

Big South Fork

Pickett State Rustic Park and Forest

Divide Rd

Station Camp Ford

9

Fork Ridge Rd

154

Charit Creek Lodge

Bandy Creek Visitor Center

297

Park Headquarters

297

Oneida

Verdun

8

Leatherwood Ford

Airport Rd

27

154

7

Confluence

To 75

Jamestown

Zenith

North White Oak Creek

6

63

New River

127

4

Mount Helen Rd

Clear Fork River

5

Allardt

52

Burnt Mill Bridge

27

Colditz Cove

2

Rugby

3

52

West Robbins Rd

1

Elgin

Peters Bridge

1 = Number of the access point as listed

④ At 10 miles south of Oneida on US27, turn west and follow the directions given earlier in the section on Access to the **Burnt Mill Bridge River Access** on the Clear Fork River. This takeout/putin is also accessible by turning north on West Robbins Road off TN52 a half mile west of Elgin, or from the west, along the Mount Helen Road that begins 7.1 miles west of Rugby.

⑤ Just 0.7 mile north of the Burnt Mill Bridge turnoff, US27 crosses the New River, the other main tributary stream creating the Big South Fork; this is the **New River Access**. There is no sign there. On the east side of the bridge on the north side of the highway, turn onto a side road and then make an immediate left on a gravel road that leads down beside the bridge to the water's edge.

⑥ The **Zenith Access** lies on North White Oak Creek, a smaller tributary of the Big South Fork. Zenith was the location of one of the old coal mining camps and coal loading stations that operated along the O&W Railroad. Take TN52 west 7.1 miles from Rugby town center and turn north on Mount Helen Road. In 5.2 miles turn left at a junction where the old Garrett Store stands to stay on the Mount Helen Road and then left again on a gravel road in another 0.2 mile. In another 0.1 mile stay right where a driveway turns left. It's then another 1.7 miles to the creek on a somewhat rough road. (The Mount Helen Road continues on from this turn down to Zenith to connect with the Burnt Mill Ford Road that takes you to the Burnt Mill Bridge River Access in 9 miles. The road becomes graveled when you stay straight at a junction at 3 miles to get on the Burnt Mill Ford Road. You'll pass the Honey Creek turnoff at 5 miles.)

⑦ There is river access at **Pine Creek/O&W Bridge** just before Leatherwood Ford. At 1.7 miles west of Oneida on TN297, turn south on Verdun Road. In another 0.6 mile turn right on the O&W Railbed, now a paved road that becomes graveled in half a mile. It's then 7.6 miles down to the O&W Bridge following the old railroad bed; the O&W stopped operating in 1954 and the tracks were pulled up. The one-lane road crosses five bridges over Pine Creek and, at this writing, is not suitable for passenger cars, but check to see if the road has been upgraded. At the bridge, steps down on the left side of the bridge provide access to the river. At one mile back up the road, you will have passed a gated side road on the left; it is accessible on foot and leads steeply down the bluff to a footpath through the woods a quarter mile to the mouth of Pine Creek. This confluence is 3 miles before Leatherwood Ford, and the O&W Bridge is 2 miles before the ford; both the creek and the bridge provide for alternative takeout and putin. Pine Creek above the putin at its confluence with the river is not runnable and should not be attempted. There is additional access to the O&W Railbed using the Toomey Road; if you're coming from the park headed east on TN297, turn right at the Terry and Terry Store and then in 0.6 mile, turn right off TN297 onto the gravel road. The Toomey Road descends to join the O&W Railbed in 3 miles; the bridge is then 4.2 miles to the right; the Toomey Road can be rutted where it descends steeply into the river gorge.

8 The **Leatherwood Ford River Access** where TN297 crosses the river is the primary takeout/putin on the Big South Fork; follow the directions given earlier in the book to this access point. If you take out at this point, you'll find changing stalls and showers near the gazebo.

9 The **Station Camp River Access** at the end of Station Camp Road is the next takeout/putin north of Leatherwood Ford. Follow the directions given in the section on Access, Facilities, and Services.

10 The next river access north is the **Blue Heron River Access** at the end of the Mine 18 Road. Follow the directions given earlier to the Blue Heron Mining Community. At Blue Heron, changing stalls and showers stand near the river access, which is at the far end of the community.

11 The **Worley River Access** is the site of an old mining community and coal loading station on the K&T Railroad. From Stearns, take KY92 west, heading toward the Yamacraw Bridge crossing of the Big South Fork. At 1.8 miles, turn south on KY791; you'll pass through the community of Smith Town. At 1.3 miles along KY791, make a sharp curve right. Just after this curve, at 1.4 miles, turn right down a gravel road; at this writing there is no sign marking this turn, so you'll have to watch for it. This steep gravel road leads quickly down toward the river; currently, the road is not suitable for passenger cars. At 1.7 miles stay to the right as a side road heads up left. At 2.0 miles you must make a hairpin turn; if that poses a problem, stay straight ahead to a turnaround from which you can then head back to the turn, approaching it straight on. Near this turnaround notice concrete steps leading down the slope from above and below the road; 165 in all, these steps connected a water tank high up the slope to a water pumping station down on the river when steam engines were used on the K&T Railroad. Continuing down the access road, you'll reach parking near the river at 2.3 miles. The takeout/putin is just ahead. You'll cross the tracks of the K&T that once led down from Stearns for the purpose of hauling timber and coal out of the area. The scenic railway out of Stearns follows the old route of the K&T, but once at the river, it turns south toward Blue Heron instead of north toward Worley. At the river, you'll still see the old concrete supports for a bridge that once spanned the river.

12 The next access north is at the **Yamacraw Bridge River Access** on the Big South Fork; follow the directions, given earlier in the Access section, to the Yamacraw Day Use Area. On the west side of the river, turn south on KY1363 and immediately turn left down a graveled road to the river's edge; the road is rough at this writing but can be negotiated by passenger cars.

13 You can reach the **Alum Ford River Access** and a boat ramp at the end of KY700; follow the directions given earlier for the Yahoo Falls Scenic Area.

14 The last access within the park is at **Big Creek** at the very northern tip of the park. From the KY700 turnoff of US27 for Yahoo Falls and Alum Ford, continue north 3.4 miles on US27; you'll pass the Stearns Ranger District Office of the Daniel Boone National Forest on the right. Turn left on Tom Roberts Road where you'll see a sign for the Sheltowee Trace. Cross railroad tracks and pass an obscure road to the left and then a more obvious road to the left. Then take the third left on a Forest Service Road in 0.6 mile from US27. Stay left at a fork, and then at 1.0 mile, when the road seems to curve right and stop, continue straight onto a gravel road; you'll see a sign for FSR663. Eventually the road curves left and right as it descends into the Big South Fork Gorge. At 3.0 miles turn right to stay on FSR663 while FSR663A continues straight. After the turn, the road becomes narrow and rocky and could be muddy in places after a recent rain; perhaps unsuitable for passenger cars. You'll enter the park boundary and descend steeply to the river and a boat ramp at 3.7 miles.

River Guide to the Big South Fork System

Distance (mi.)	Difficulty (Int. Scale)	Avg. Drop (ft./mi.)	Season	Comments
Peters Bridge to Rugby Access (Clear Fork River)				
6	I–II	7	W, Sp	short drops; long pools
Rugby Access to Burnt Mill Bridge (Clear Fork River)				
10.5	II–III	12	F, W, Sp	numerous boulders; moderate rapids; water increases below White Oak Creek
White Oak Creek to Burnt Mill Bridge (White Oak Creek, Clear Fork River)				
11	II	13	W, Sp	no major rapids
Burnt Mill Bridge to Leatherwood Ford (Clear Fork River, Big South Fork)				
11	III–IV	20	F, W, S	serious whitewater; Clear Fork joins with New River to create Big South Fork in river gorge; major rapids: *First Drop, Double Falls, Washing Machine, The Ell, Honey Creek, Rions Eddy, Jakes Hole, O&W Rapids*
New River to Leatherwood Ford (New River, Big South Fork)				
15.5	I–IV	14	F, W, Sp	first 6 miles easy on New River but water has silt and mine drainage, II-III ledges before joining with Clear Fork to create Big South Fork; then major rapids: *Double Falls, Washing Machine, The Ell, Honey Creek, Rions Eddy, Jakes Hole, O&W Rapids*

Distance (mi.)	Difficulty (Int. Scale)	Avg. Drop (ft./mi.)	Season	Comments
Zenith to Leatherwood Ford				
(North White Oak Creek, Big South Fork)				
8.5	II–III	22	W, Sp	short rapids; gradient fluctuates
Leatherwood Ford to Station Camp				
(Big South Fork)				
8	II–IV	5	F, W, Sp	relatively clear channel; moderate waves; one major rapid: *Angel Falls* (portage at 3000 or more cfs)
Station Camp to Blue Heron				
(Big South Fork)				
19	II–IV	5	F, W, Sp	relatively clear channel; moderate waves; major rapids: *Big Shoals, Devils Jump* (portage at 3000 or more cfs)
Blue Heron to Worley				
(Big South Fork)				
2.5	II	5	F, W, Sp	relatively clear channel
Worley to Yamacraw Bridge				
(Big South Fork)				
2.5	II	5	F, W, Sp	relatively clear channel
Yamacraw Bridge to Alum Ford				
(Big South Fork)				
5	I–II	5-0	F, W, Sp	clear channel; lake water begins
Alum Ford to Big Creek				
(Big South Fork)				
4	I	0	Year-round	clear channel; lake water

Recommended Minimum and Maximum Flow

Minimums represent water needed to paddle the stream; maximums are guidelines on which to base a judgment of your own abilities; numbers are based on Leatherwood Ford gage and are expressed in cubic feet per second (cfs).

River Section	Minimum	Maximum
Clear Fork before Burnt Mill Bridge:		
Canoes and kayaks	600 cfs	5000 cfs
Rafts	1200 cfs	15,000 cfs
White Oak Creek:		
Canoes and kayaks	1000 cfs	7000 cfs
Rafts	2000 cfs	10,000 cfs
Big South Fork from Burnt Mill Bridge to Leatherwood Ford:		
Canoes and kayaks	600 cfs	3000 cfs
Rafts	1100 cfs	10,000 cfs
New River:		
Canoes and kayaks	600 cfs	5000 cfs
Rafts	1200 cfs	10,000 cfs
North White Oak Creek:		
Canoes and kayaks	1800 cfs	10,000 cfs
Rafts	Too narrow for rafting	
Big South Fork downstream from Leatherwood Ford:		
Canoes and kayaks	150 cfs	3000 cfs
Rafts	400 cfs	15,000 cfs

Road Bicycling

All of the highways and back roads open to passenger car traffic are open and suitable for bicycling. Those that are not paved can be rough and have loose gravel; you will be better off using a mountain bike or similar type of bicycle with knobby tires on the dirt or gravel roads.

Riding TN297 through the park is quite an experience; the paved road dips into the gorge to Leatherwood Ford and back up. Within the park, TN297 has good shoulders for easy biking. You can park at either the West Entrance Trailhead, or at the East Entrance and then ride between these two points for a trip of 7.3 miles one-way. The road in and out of the gorge area is a difficult one, so you'll need to be in good shape to make the trip. Because of the unrelenting steepness and curving nature of the road down to the river, and because the shoulders get a little narrow in the gorge, it is advisable that you walk your bicycle when descending; at least make sure you have good brakes.

In the Kentucky portion of the park, you can ride from the town of Stearns on KY1651 south to Revelo and turn right on KY742 and ride down to the Blue Heron Mining Community for a trip of 9.3 miles one-way; there is no shoulder to speak of and some parts are steep, so be careful. You can add a side trip along the way by biking out to the Devils Jump and Blue Heron Overlooks on the Overlooks Road, which also has no shoulder. If you want to avoid the tough ride back out of the gorge, you can combine a bike ride down to Blue Heron with a train ride back to Stearns on the Big South Fork Scenic Railway; purchase your one-way ticket and check the departure times at the railway office and gift shop in Stearns; get permission to take your bike on the train.

You'll find easier riding if you stay in the rim area and don't descend into the river gorge. You can begin at the Bandy Creek Visitor Center in Tennessee and head back out to TN297 and turn west, riding the highway all the way to TN154 and then heading north to the Middle Creek area and Pickett State Rustic Park and Forest, 16 miles one-way; TN297 to TN154 has ample shoulders. In Kentucky, you can ride from Stearns to the Devils Jump and Blue Heron Overlooks and back for a roundtrip ride of 16.6 miles.

You'll need to keep your bicycle in good shape to handle the ascents and descents. Watch for traffic; some drivers in the region are not yet accustomed to bike riders. Always wear a helmet.

Mountain Biking

Along with hiking, horseback riding, and river paddling, mountain biking is quickly becoming a major outdoor activity in the BSFNRRA. The park offers some of the best opportunity for mountain biking in the Southeast along old roads, horse trails, and a few routes specifically designed for mountain bikes.

If you have a mountain bike or other bicycle suitable for off-road use, you can ride the Duncan Hollow and Collier Ridge Loop mountain bike trails constructed by the local Big South Fork Bicycle Club. In addition to these trails, you may also ride many old dirt roads that wind through the park in the adjacent area; if a road is overgrown with trees and brush or if it is blazed for hiking, it is not open to bicycles.

Safety

While exploring some of the unmarked roads in the park, you'll need to pay attention to where you are; it's easy to get lost. You should get topographic maps of the area you'll be riding in, available at the visitor centers; many of the old roads appear on the topos.

Mountain bikers may also use horse trails, but bicycles are not permitted on designated hiking trails; you may not even walk a bicycle down a hiking trail unless it is designated as a multiple-use trail. If you ride the horse trails, stop your bike and move to the side any time you encounter horses to allow them to get by. Stand still and speak in a normal voice; do not call out, which would startle the horses. You can get a trail map at the visitor centers that shows both hiking and horse trails.

Plan your route ahead of time and study the trail and road connections. Ask the rangers about the current conditions of the trails and about any problem areas, such as stream crossings and rock ledges that are difficult to negotiate. You should let the rangers know where you are going, especially if you are exploring old roads; at least let a friend or member of your family know where you intend to be so they can contact the park staff if you get into trouble and do not return when expected. It is best to ride with someone; then if one of you is injured, the other person will be there to attend to the injuries and to go for help.

Keep your bike in good shape to handle the rough roads and steep ascents and descents. Always wear a helmet. Take plenty of drinking water along or be prepared to purify creek water if you intend to stay in the backcountry for long; water is also available at Bandy Creek, Leatherwood Ford, Charit Creek Lodge, and Blue Heron. If you are camping in the backcountry, you of course must pack along all the necessary equipment for spending the night outside.

Mountain Bike Routes of the Big South Fork

1 The 5.0-mile **Duncan Hollow Loop** mountain bike trail begins at the Bandy Creek Visitor Center, where you can get a map and description of the two designated mountain bike trails. From the visitor center, the trail heads into the campground and takes Duncan Hollow Road north and then turns west on By-Pass Road; the bike trail leaves the road to loop through the woods and reconnect with By-Pass Road and then return along Duncan Hollow Road; the route is marked with posts that have orange lettering and arrows. A proposed addition will be a John Litton Loop south off Duncan Hollow Road.

2 The 7.3-mile **Collier Ridge Loop** mountain bike trail also begins at the Bandy Creek Visitor Center; heading west on the Bandy Creek Road past the Lora E. Blevins Farmstead, the bike trail turns south off the gravel road to loop through the woods, fording the north and south branches of Bandy Creek. Nearing TN297, the trail turns off to the right to parallel the highway on a rough track for advanced bikers; if you are not experienced, you should continue straight to TN297 and ride the highway to pick up the trail again on the right beyond this advanced section. The loop route is marked with posts that have orange arrows and also white arrows on brown metal signs.

3 There is a 1.5-mile **West Bandy Creek Trail** off the Bandy Creek Road that has been used in bike races; this trail is often narrow and steep and not for beginners. Ride down the road 2.7 miles from the Bandy Creek Visitor Center or 0.6 mile in from the West Entrance Trailhead and watch for the trail on the north side of the road; the trail circles east to come out one mile down the Bandy Creek Road. The trail is flagged with strips of blue plastic, tied on branches and around trees, which will probably be replaced with more permanent signs soon. Watch for the flags through several turns. Toward the end, turn right to emerge on Bandy Creek Road.

Mountain Biking Routes of the Big South Fork

N W E S

0   2   4 miles

27

Yahoo Falls Scenic Area

Alum Ford

700

Marshes Siding

Whitley City

92

Yamacraw Bridge

To Monticello

92

1651

92

Stearns

Revelo

1363

742

1651

92

Blue Heron

Pine Knot

11

11

Laurel Ridge Road

Waters Cemetery Rd

Bear Creek Scenic Area

1470

12

KENTUCKY
TENNESSEE

Big South Fork

Station Camp

11

Terry Cemetery Rd

14

Pickett State Rustic Park and Forest

Divide Rd

13

Charit Creek Lodge

154

15

1

Bandy Creek Visitor Center

4

Fork Ridge Rd

3

Park Headquarters

297

Oneida

Verdun

West Entrance Trailhead

2

10

297

5

9

27

154

6

8

O&W Bridge

7

To 75

Jamestown

Zenith

63

127

Mount Helen Rd

Allardt

Burnt Mill Bridge

27

Colditz Cove

52

Rugby

52

Elgin

Peters Bridge

❶ = Number of the mountain biking route as listed

4 If you are a beginner to mountain biking, you may want to first try the loop formed by the **Bandy Creek Road** and **TN297**; part of the route is over a gravel road and so gives you some experience riding unpaved track. Start from the visitor center and head west on Bandy Creek Road; in 0.2 mile it becomes gravel, and you'll then have a 3.1-mile ride on unpaved road to TN297 at the West Entrance Trailhead. Turn east on TN297 and ride back to the Bandy Creek Road and the visitor center for a loop ride of 9 miles.

5 From the Bandy Creek area, you can also ride the 16.1-mile **North White Oak Loop**, starting at the Bandy Creek Equestrian Trailhead. This is one of the popular routes for bicycles that use horse trails. This route includes a 1.5-mile side trip to an overlook of Leatherwood Ford. If you only ride to the Leatherwood Overlook, it's a ride of 5.4 miles one way. Check the horse trail descriptions for details.

6 You can also ride the **Gar Blevins Trail** which follows the old Gar Blevins Road that cuts through the middle of the North White Oak Loop for a 3.9-mile ride to North White Oak Creek Overlook. The road begins south off TN297 one mile east of the West Entrance Trailhead or 3 miles west of the east end of Bandy Creek Road; the first several yards are paved, and you may park there, but stay to the side so as not to block access to the trail.

7 The **Coyle Branch Trail** south from the North White Oak Loop along the old Coyle Branch Road descends to the old O&W Railroad bed in 5.1 miles; be aware the descent can be rough and rocky. In addition to accessing the North White Oak Loop at the Bandy Creek Equestrian Trailhead, there is a second access 1.2 miles west of the Bandy Creek Road; a road there heads south to quickly intersect with the North White Oak Loop, where you'll turn left to the Coyle Branch Trail. At this access point, the old road is paved for a few yards before the trail leads into the woods; you may park there, but stay to the side.

8 You can also reach the O&W Railbed along the 6-mile **Gernt Trail** that begins at the Cumberland Valley Trailhead on a gravel road on the east side of the Hitching Post Grocery that's 1 mile outside the west park boundary; the store is operated by a member of the Slaven family. Following the Gernt Road, the trail heads south toward North White Oak Creek, descending to the railbed at the site of the old community of

Gernt, which was a mining and lumber camp along the O&W where the Gernt family, German settlers in the region, had interests. A good overlook lies 0.1 mile beyond the start of the descent. This can be a tough descent, rocky and rough.

9 The old **O&W Railbed** is fun for mountain biking. You can ride the gravel road that now follows the railbed down from Verdun 8.2 miles to the O&W Bridge; check the directions given in the section on paddling. It's a great ride that crosses five bridges over Pine Creek and passes between rock walls; you should walk your bikes over the bridges that are wooden because there are gaps in the planking that can catch a tire. Keep in mind that at least for the present this road is maintained by the county for vehicular traffic. It is also a popular route for four-wheel driving—not too bad during the week, but on weekends you could be eating a lot of dust. (Several studies have recommended that the road be converted to a hiking/bicycling trail within the park; so at some future time, the road at the boundary of the park, or closer to the river, may be closed and used only for hiking and bicycling.) Once you are down to the river, you can walk your bike across the O&W Bridge and continue riding on the old railbed about a mile to a difficult ford of North White Oak Creek; here you'll leave most traffic behind and enjoy more solitude along 6 miles of the old railbed to Zenith, passing the Coyle Branch Road and the Gernt Road along the way and fording Laurel Creek; the route is likely to have many long, deep mud holes, which makes it even more fun. If you intend to come out at Zenith, you must ford North White Oak Creek again and follow the gravel road up to the Mount Helen Road; check the section on paddling for directions. The railbed west of Zenith becomes overgrown.

10 There's also a 2-mile roundtrip ride out to the **O&W Overlook** along a dirt road on the south side of TN297; the road begins just inside the park from the east entrance sign. This road crosses private land before entering the park and is signed for no trespassing to prevent hunters and others from venturing into the woods. You may bike up this road, but do not leave the roadway. At the overlook, from the top of a bluff called "Yellow Cliffs," you'll have a panoramic view that includes the O&W Railroad Bridge over the Big South Fork. Be careful; there are no railings at the overlook. A proposed East Rim Trail for mountain bikes will connect O&W Overlook with Sunset Overlook and the East Rim Overlook Road.

11 From the Middle Creek Trailhead on the west side of the park, you can ride Divide Road, joining the **Long Trail** for horses, into the Kentucky portion of the park. (Divide Road becomes the Peters Mountain Road at the state line.) Then take Laurel Ridge Road, following the horse-head blaze through a couple of turns, to Bald Knob and then turn down the Waters Cemetery Road and follow the horse trail northeast to Blue Heron, a ride of 25 miles; check the horse trail description for details. So that bicycles can avoid the steep descent and ford of the river on the horse trail, it has been proposed that the hiking trail leading to the tram bridge at Blue Heron be designated multiple use and that you be allowed to walk your bike across the bridge; check with the park rangers for whether that change has been made. Once you get to Blue Heron, you'll need a shuttle to pick you up, unless you intend to ride back. The shuttle can meet you in Stearns if you want to ride the Big South Fork Scenic Railway one way out of Blue Heron.

12 You can make a loop of 30 miles on the **Big Island Branch Loop** off the Long Trail by turning off Laurel Ridge Road on the Laurel Hill Road and following the horse trail down to Big Island and on to Station Camp Creek, up the creek to Charit Creek Lodge, and then along Fork Ridge Road back to Divide Road and the Middle Creek Trailhead; check the horse trail description. But be aware that the portion of the loop along the river is soft and sandy and used frequently by horses, so you'll often be pushing your bike and standing aside. That section of the horse trail is scheduled to be rerouted at some future time. You might want to do this in winter when there is less horse traffic. Also be aware the descent into the river gorge and ascent back out are steep.

13 The **Hatfield Ridge Branch Loop** off the Long Trail forms a 14.4-mile circuit; turn south off Divide Road at Three Forks on the Terry Cemetery Road, then at 1.9 miles, turn south on a side road that's also the Hatfield Ridge Trail to connect with the Hatfield Ridge Loop to Charit Creek Lodge. You can then ride back along Fork Ridge Road to Divide Road and the Middle Creek Trailhead.

14 From Charit Creek Lodge, you can ride the 9.9-mile **Hatfield Ridge Loop**, which is a horse trail, first following the Station Camp Creek Trail toward the Big South Fork, fording the creek several times, and then turning up Hatfield Ridge to circle back to the lodge with views along the way, including a side trail to the Charit Creek Overlook.

15 Or from the lodge, you can ride the **Station Camp Creek** and **Duncan Hollow Trails** to Bandy Creek and back along the **Jacks Ridge**, **Black House Branch**, and **Charit Creek Lodge Trails**, for a 12.7-mile loop ride to Bandy Creek and back. You can, of course, also start at the Bandy Creek Visitor Center and ride to Charit Creek Lodge and back. Be aware there are a number of crossings of Station Camp Creek. You can avoid the crossings by riding up the Charit Creek Lodge Trail 1.5 miles from the lodge and taking the Fork Ridge Trail east to connect with the Duncan Hollow Trail, although at this writing the steep descent into the river gorge is blocked by fallen trees; that section has been designated for rerouting.

Climbing and Rappelling

The BSFNRRA with its walls of sandstone offers exciting opportunities for rock climbing and rappelling. But remember these are inherently dangerous activities; you should be experienced or be with someone who is experienced before climbing or rappelling in the park.

The park has no officially designated places for this activity. One place for climbing and rappelling is the O&W Overlook, which you reach by walking the mile-long dirt road to the south off TN297 just inside the East Entrance to the park. But the rock wall there is quite high and intimidating. So you might want to stay with shorter rock walls that you'll find virtually everywhere in the park.

In Kentucky, on the Mine 18 Road down to Blue Heron, just after the road curves left where there has been some construction work to stabilize the road, a good climbing wall stands up the slope to the left of the road; watch for an area on the left after the rock wall where you can park and walk back up the road. The Twin Arches/Charit Creek Loop offers a variety of climbs on the section of trail from Twin Arches counterclockwise toward Jakes Place where it passes along a rock wall, but do not climb on the arches themselves. If you want to hike into the backcountry to climb, you'll find good rock in the No Business Creek area.

You should not climb at developed overlooks or any other high-use areas where you might endanger other visitors. Climbing on Twin Arches, Yahoo Falls, or any other special geologic formation is not permitted, to prevent damage to these structures and to protect their scenic value for other visitors. You are not permitted to damage a rock face in any way, so you may not drive climbing nails or spikes into the rock walls.

Always climb with others and let someone else know where you are and what you are doing in case of an accident; filing a plan with the rangers is always a good idea. You should have all the proper climbing and safety equipment.

Caving

The BSFNRRA abounds in rock shelters where light penetrates all the way to the back of the openings. These can be explored by anyone agile enough to scramble around boulders, but use caution. Do not dig for artifacts under the rock shelters; such artifacts are protected by federal law. You may not camp or start fires in the shelters.

The park lacks true caves because the rock is sandstone. The river has only recently eroded down to limestone, the rock in which deep caves are formed. Station Camp, Parch Corn, and No Business Creeks have reached the limestone in their lower portions where they meet the river, and so perhaps there are caves in that region, but none have been recorded. If you do find a cave, explore it only if you are an experienced spelunker (or are with someone who is experienced) and have all the necessary caving and safety equipment. Report the location of any cave you find to the park rangers; you must obtain a permit before entering a cave. Always cave with others and let someone else know where you are and what you are doing in case of an accident.

Most abandoned coal mines in the park have been closed or gated. If you happen upon one that is open, do not enter because of the unstable nature of mines and because of dangerous gases that may collect in a mine. Report any open mine to the park rangers.

Swimming and Snorkeling

You'll find a swimming pool at the Bandy Creek Campground. In addition, there are a number of spots in the Big South Fork River and its tributary creeks where you can wade and swim at low water, although there are no places specifically designated for swimming in the river system.

The Leatherwood Ford River Access is a fine place for splashing around. You'll find nearby changing stalls and showers for river users. Other traditional places to swim are the Burnt Mill Bridge, Rugby, and Peters Bridge Access on the Clear Fork River, the Gentlemen's Swimming Hole at Rugby on the Clear Fork, and the Station Camp and Blue Heron access points on the Big South Fork.

At low water when the river runs clear, you can also have fun snorkeling while looking for the various fish and mollusk species that inhabit the river system. The pools around Leatherwood Ford and Blue Heron are suitable for snorkeling.

You should only swim in the river and creeks at low water. Even then, you should be careful; the river possesses deep pools and strong currents; drownings are possible and have occurred. Holes, rocks, undercurrents, and ledges can make you fall and perhaps entrap feet and legs. You should not swim above rapids, where you might

Wading in Station Camp Creek

get caught in the current and pulled into the rocks. Never swim alone, and never enter the river or streams at high water when you will be unable to fight the current. Do not dive into the river; there may be rocks hidden beneath the water's surface. Swim in the river and creeks at your own risk.

Picnicking

The recreation area contains fifteen developed picnic areas with tables and grills. Restrooms are available at Bandy Creek, Leatherwood Ford, and Blue Heron; other sites usually have chemical toilets for use in spring, summer, and fall.

Designated Picnic Areas in the Big South Fork

Bandy Creek Visitor Center
Leatherwood Ford River Access
Station Camp River Access
Twin Arches Trailhead
Rugby River Access
Gentlemen's Swimming Hole
  Trailhead
Burnt Mill Bridge River Access

Honey Creek Overlook
Peters Bridge River Access
Blue Heron Mining Community
Bear Creek Scenic Area
Yamacraw Day Use Area
Yahoo Falls Scenic Area
Alum Ford River Access
Joe Branch Picnic Area

Directions are given in earlier sections of this book to these locations, with the exception of the Joe Branch Picnic Area. To get to that picnic area, drive west from the Honey Creek turnoff on Burnt Mill Ford Road 1.9 miles to a left turn when the road becomes the paved Mount Helen Road. At the turn the road is signed the Honey Creek Loop Road, but that road soon turns off to the left and the main road continues on as part of the Mount Helen Road. At 2.8 miles from that turn, the road passes the Mount Helen United Baptist Church and curves sharply to the right where you'll see the beginning of the gravel Joe Branch Road on the left into the picnic area. (From the west, you can get to this point by turning north off TN52 on the Mount Helen Road 5.2 miles to a junction at the old Garrett Store and then bear right as the Mount Helen Road continues left; from this junction, it's 1.6 miles to the Joe Branch Road.)

As you head down the gravel road, you'll pass the Mount Helen Cemetery and just beyond, at a fork, stay right and then stay straight where a side road leads to the right. Halfway along the road, curve sharply right as the trace of an old route continues straight for a short distance. The road makes a steep drop into a hollow and then ascends. When you arrive at the picnic area at 2.4 miles, you'll find picnic tables, grills, and hitching rails for horses.

The unimproved continuation of the road is used for horseback riding. To the right, a dirt road passes an unimproved road to the right and more picnic tables on the left; the road continues unimproved into the woods. Behind these picnic tables and grills on the left, you can walk down the hill on a track, possibly overgrown but usually mowed, to a pond with bluegill and smallmouth bass. Bring along a picnic lunch and a fishing pole and spend a leisurely afternoon.

There is also a picnic table at the White Oak Creek River Access, just west of the bridge over White Oak Creek outside the park. Watch for other picnic areas to be established as road access is improved into other areas of the park.

The river boardwalks at Leatherwood Ford offer benches and platforms where you can have lunch beside the river.

In addition to developed areas, you'll find picturesque locations on the river and shaded streams that are ideal for picnicking. Huge boulders at stream-side make excellent spots for laying out a lunch. Make sure you carry out all trash. Be careful near the water and keep an eye on children; falling in the water can mean loss of life at such places as Angel Falls where swift water sweeps past undercut boulders. Watch for snakes that may be lying on rocks in the sun at stream's edge.

Picnicking at the Big South Fork

Sightseeing

I f you want a leisurely visit to the park, there's plenty of opportunity for just sightseeing. Stop by the Bandy Creek Visitor Center for orientation and information.

The drive down to Leatherwood Ford on TN297 and a stroll along the river boardwalks lets you experience the river in the Tennessee portion of the park. A visit to the Blue Heron Mining Community in Kentucky along KY742 and Mine 18 Road offers a step back in time to the days of coal mining along the Big South Fork.

If you are interested in the history of the region, you can hike some of the short trails mentioned in the section on the history of the Big South Fork. You can also drive beyond the Bandy Creek Visitor Center to reach the Lora E. Blevins Farmstead and the Katie Blevins Cemetery, also described in the history section.

You can also take relatively easy short walks to the waterfalls, arches, and rock shelters described in the geology section of this book.

Then there are the various park overlooks that give you an opportunity to get wide-ranging views of the river gorge. In the geology section, you are directed to

Stopping at Leatherwood Ford Overlook

the Devils Jump Overlook in the Kentucky portion of the park and to the Honey Creek Overlook in Tennessee to study the creation of the Big South Fork Gorge. Other viewing areas include the Blue Heron, Bear Creek, Dick Gap, and East Rim Overlooks. Some undeveloped overlooks, like the Sunset, Leatherwood, and Angel Falls Overlooks, require some walking; there are many other overlooks not mentioned in the accompanying chart that you'll discover while hiking or riding in the backcountry. Most of them do not have railings, so use caution.

Scenic Overlooks of the Big South Fork

Overlook	View/Directions
❶ Devils Jump	BSF Gorge and Devils Jump Rapids; take Overlooks Road off Mine 18 Road on the way to Blue Heron.
❷ Blue Heron	BSF Gorge in the vicinity of Blue Heron, no views of the Blue Heron Community; continue on Overlooks Road from the Devils Jump Overlook to the road's end, and then walk the paved trail to the gorge rim.
❸ Dick Gap	Blue Heron Mining Community across the river; follow the directions given in the history section toward the old Beaty oil well, but before Bald Knob Road and just after the Beech Grove Baptist Church, turn left down the Waters Cemetery Road and in 0.3 mile turn left on a road that leads to the overlook parking in 1.0 mile; it's then a 0.3-mile walk to the overlook.
❹ Bear Creek	Meandering BSF; as KY742 becomes Mine 18 Road, turn south toward the Bear Creek Scenic Area and follow signs 3.6 miles to the overlook parking and then walk the graveled trail to the overlook.

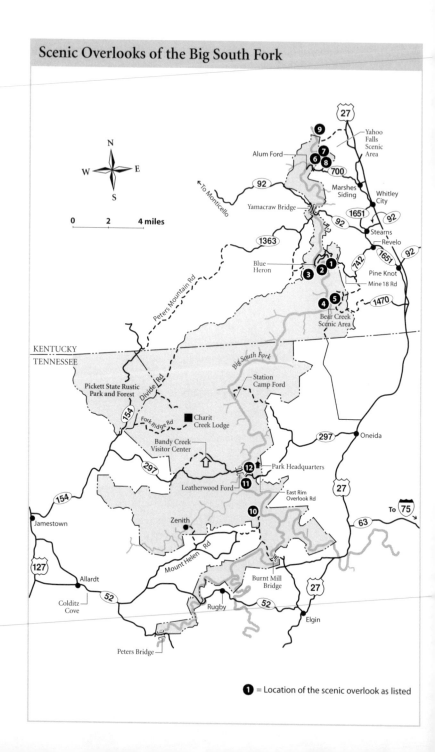

Scenic Overlooks of the Big South Fork

N
W — E
S

0   2   4 miles

To Monticello

27
Yahoo Falls Scenic Area
9
Alum Ford
7
6 8
700
Marshes Siding
Whitley City
92
Yamacraw Bridge
92
1651
92
Stearns
Revelo
1363
Blue Heron
1
3 2
742
1651
92
Pine Knot
Mine 18 Rd
4 5
1470
Bear Creek Scenic Area

Peters Mountain Rd

KENTUCKY
TENNESSEE

Big South Fork

Station Camp Ford

Divide Rd

Pickett State Rustic Park and Forest
154
Fork Ridge Rd
Charit Creek Lodge

297
Oneida

Bandy Creek Visitor Center
12
Park Headquarters
297
11
Leatherwood Ford
East Rim Overlook Rd

154
27

Jamestown
Zenith
10
To 75
63

127
Mount Helen Rd

Allardt
52
Burnt Mill Bridge
27
Colditz Cove
Rugby
52
Elgin

Peters Bridge

1 = Location of the scenic overlook as listed

5 **Split Bow Arch**

An arch formed by joint widening and headward erosion; you'll see the overlook to the right as you enter the Bear Creek Scenic Area 0.1 mile before the Bear Creek Overlook parking.

6 **Lake Cumberland**

Waters of the lake backed up into the BSF Gorge; from the Yahoo Falls Scenic Area Trailhead, walk down the road a short distance and turn right down some steps to the overlook.

7 **Yahoo Creek**

The confluence of the creek with the BSF; from the Yahoo Falls Trailhead, walk the Topside Loop a short distance to a side path on the left that leads down to the overlook.

8 **Yahoo Falls**

The 113-foot waterfall; continue on the Topside Loop for 0.2 mile to the overlook on the left; you can then continue on the loop to cross the creek above the falls and reach a similar overlook on the other side of the waterfall.

9 **Buzzard Rock**

One of the best views of the BSF Gorge, with the waters of Lake Cumberland, an undeveloped overlook. Follow the directions given earlier toward the river access at Big Creek in the section on paddling. Then on FSR663, 2.4 miles from US27, watch for a dirt road to the right. Unless you have four-wheel drive and plenty of clearance, park here so that you do not block the road. Then walk up the road for half a mile to its end, staying with the main road where side roads take off. At the end, follow the footpath down to Buzzard Rock, a bare rock promontory that has an expansive view.

❿ Honey Creek

Bare rock walls and the BSF Gorge; from the Burnt Mill River Access, continue on the Burnt Mill Ford Road 3.4 miles and turn right to reach the overlook in 0.8 mile.

⓫ East Rim

BSF Gorge; turn left off TN297 0.5 mile inside the park's East Entrance, drive to end of the road, and walk down to the overlook.

⓬ Leatherwood Ford

BSF Gorge and the bridge at Leatherwood Ford; from the East Rim Trailhead walk the Leatherwood Ford Loop clockwise 0.4 mile to a 0.1-mile side trail that leads to the overlook.

The following overlooks are along hiking and horse trails:

Blue Heron Tipple

The tipple and tram bridge over the river; from the mining community, hike the Blue Heron Loop clockwise 0.7 mile to where the main trail turns right and an unofficial side trail leads left to the undeveloped overlook; or you can reach this point on the loop by taking the side trail on the right from the developed Blue Heron Overlook that drops down to the Blue Heron Loop and then turn right on the loop for 0.2 mile.

Catawba

BSF Gorge from the west and Blue Heron Community in the distance; at the Blue Heron Mining Community, walk across the river on the tram bridge and turn south on the hiking trail 1.6 miles to the overlook on the left.

O&W

BSF Gorge and the O&W Railroad Bridge; just inside the park's East Entrance, turn left on an old road and walk 1.1 miles to the gorge rim; undeveloped.

Sunset

BSF Gorge and confluence of North White Oak Creek; park at the East Rim Trailhead on the road to the East Rim Overlook, and walk south on the Sunset Overlook Trail 1.3 miles to the edge of the gorge; undeveloped.

North White Oak Creek

Gorge of the BSF tributary where the O&W Railroad once operated; hike, horseback ride, or bike the 16.1-mile North White Oak Loop from the Bandy Creek Equestrian Trailhead or from access on TN297, to about halfway along the loop; or you can also follow the Gar Blevins Trail 3.9 miles one way through the middle of the loop.

Leatherwood

BSF Gorge and Leatherwood Ford; take a 1.5-mile side trail off the North White Oak Loop east to the overlook.

Angel Falls

Probably the best view in the park of the BSF Gorge; from Leatherwood Ford, hike the John Muir Trail north on the west side of the river 3 miles to turn right on the Grand Gap Loop to reach the view; undeveloped.

Grand Gap

Distant view of the Angel Falls Rapids; hike the Grand Gap Loop counterclockwise 1.2 miles from the junction with the John Muir Trail to where you switchback down to the gorge rim for a short side path to the view; undeveloped.

John Muir

No Business Creek Valley; backpack the John Muir Trail 26 miles north from Leatherwood Ford into the backcountry, or walk 7 miles east on the John Muir Trail from its crossing of Divide Road in the Middle Creek area; for a shorter route, walk Chestnut Ridge Road off Peters Mountain Road in Kentucky to a junction with the John Muir Trail in 2.0 miles, the overlook is to the left in another 0.6 mile; undeveloped.

Charit Creek	Charit Creek Lodge; hike, bike, or horseback ride the Hatfield Ridge Loop clockwise 1 mile to a half-mile side trail south to the overlook.
Station Camp East	BSF Gorge; from the Station Camp East Trailhead, walk right on the Pilot/Wines Loop for 0.1 mile to a fork and take the right fork 0.9 mile to the overlook; undeveloped.
East Laurel	Gorge of Laurel Fork on North White Oak Creek; from the Cumberland Valley Trailhead, follow the Gernt Trail 2.7 miles to where the trail turns left down into the gorge and go straight another 0.1 mile to the end of the old road and a side path to the right to the overlook; undeveloped.

Photography

The Big South Fork region possesses a geologic landscape with dramatic scenes that include the river gorge, waterfalls, arches, chimneys, and rock shelters. You'll also find old log cabins and barns, weathered gravestones, and abandoned railroad bridges that span the rivers and streams.

The best times to photograph are early mornings and late afternoons with their soft light and long shadows that give a sense of depth to your pictures. Some of the easily accessible gorge overlooks, such as the East Rim and Bear Creek Overlooks, face west, so you'll probably want to visit those in the mornings unless you want a shot of sunset over the gorge. The Devils Jump and Blue Heron Overlooks face south.

The middle part of the day, when the most light penetrates to the forest floor, is perhaps the best time for photographing the more subtle beauties of the park—wildflowers and wildlife, light on water, patterns in the rocks, leaves, and trees.

Those who can take advantage of the opportunities for photography range from the beginner with a simple camera who can't miss with an overlook shot to the professional or experienced amateur who captures a flitting bird or the soft steps of a cascading stream. Even the casual visitor will bring home pictures to show friends and perhaps display on a wall.

Picture-perfect view from Devils Jump Overlook

When stepping off a trail to take a photograph, leave as little impact as possible. Avoid trampling wildflowers and ferns or causing erosion on a steep bank while getting to your perfect picture.

Other Activities

Four-Wheel Drive, ATV, and Trail Bike Riding

The BSFNRRA has old dirt roads where four-wheel drive, all-terrain vehicle, and trail bike riding is permitted. This activity is limited to roads within the adjacent rim area; if a road is overgrown with trees and brush or if it is blazed for hiking, horseback riding, or mountain biking, it is not considered an existing road and so is not open to vehicular traffic. Such vehicles are not allowed in the gorge area.

While traveling a road in the park, do not go beyond any gate, post, berm, cable, or sign intended to restrict access. To protect the environment, travel is restricted to existing roads—do not turn off into any open wildlife plot or agricultural field and do not attempt to blaze a trail through the forest. Do not turn off on any hiking, horseback, or bicycling trail designated solely for such use. Act responsibly and safely while respecting the rights of others to use the park undisturbed. Whenever you encounter horseback riders on the roads, pull to the side, stop, and shut down your engine so as not to scare the horses and to allow them to pass by.

You must be at least 16 years of age to drive any motorized vehicle in the park. Vehicles that are not licensed for highway use are restricted from using publicly maintained roads and highways within the park, including county roads that may appear to be just old dirt roads. Unlicensed vehicles in Tennessee must have a Tennessee Department of Revenue sticker on the vehicle, available from any Tennessee County Clerk. Such stickers are not required for Kentucky vehicles at this time. Operators from outside Tennessee should carry registration or ownership documentation. Such vehicles are required to have headlights and taillights in use from a half hour after sunset to a half hour before sunrise. Check with park rangers for additional rules, regulations, and safety tips.

Hunting, Fishing, and Trapping

Hunting is allowed in the BSFNRRA with valid state licenses and subject to state and federal regulations. Keep in mind that the park is in two states;

you must have a license for the state in which you are hunting. Also be aware the seasons vary; while there may be hunting in the Tennessee portion of the park, there may be no hunting in the Kentucky portion, or vice versa. Check with the Kentucky Department of Fish and Wildlife Resources and the Tennessee Wildlife Resources Agency for the seasons, species limits, and state regulations; addresses and telephone numbers are listed in Appendix A.

You should check with the park rangers for any federal regulations that apply, especially for the transport of guns. Vertical yellow "Safety Zone" signs designate the boundary of areas where no hunting is allowed. Remember that others are also permitted to use the park during hunting seasons; be on the lookout for backcountry hikers, mountain bikers, and horseback riders. To avoid contact with nonhunters, keep to the backcountry where fewer people go, and stay at least 200 feet away from backcountry trails. Always wear blaze orange during hunting season.

Fishing in the park is subject to state and federal regulations. You must have valid state licenses. Keep in mind that the park resides in two states; you must have a license for the state in which you are fishing. Commercial fishing is not allowed. Check with the Kentucky Department of Fish and Wildlife Resources and the Tennessee Wildlife Resources Agency for creel and size limits and other state regulations.

At one time, trapping animals for furs was a way of obtaining supplemental income for those living on subsistence farms in the area. But trapping is no longer economically viable due to the low price for furs. Even so, trapping is allowed in the BSFNRRA subject to Tennessee and Kentucky regulations. You must have a license to trap for the state in which you are operating. River otters and spotted skunks are rare and must not be taken. Do not set traps on trails or in other areas that will be frequented by people. All traps must be visited once a day and any animals removed. Check with the Kentucky Department of Fish and Wildlife Resources and the Tennessee Wildlife Resources Agency for the furbearer seasons, species limits, and other state regulations.

Special Events, Programs, and Organizations

The BSFNRRA has a number of programs in which the public can participate, from educational presentations for school groups and campfire talks for the park's overnight visitors to opportunities for the public to donate time and resources in support of the park. In addition, there are outside community and conservation groups working for the park that you may join and/or support. For the park's programs, contact the Bandy Creek Visitor Center for information. For outside groups, contact the individual group. Addresses and phone numbers are listed in the back of this book.

Environmental Education Program

The park staff provides a variety of programs in environmental education for school groups. Programs presented in area schools include archaeological resource protection, survival skills, recycling, litter problems, food chains and food webs, snakes, mammals, and fighting wildfires. Programs presented to school groups that come to the park include Native American habitation, trees, river safety, clean water, and guided hikes introducing students to the park's resources. Schools and individual teachers may request these programs for their classes and may also ask for a program to be designed for their specific needs.

Longhunter Program

A park ranger in traditional longhunter dress of the 1780s depicts the early exploration of the region. The longhunter discusses how a person or family group might survive in the open at a time when the only resources were the forest and what the people were able to bring with them. This program is available to school groups, scouts, and community groups and at times is presented at campfire programs.

Campfire Programs

Between Memorial Day and Labor Day, the park staff presents campfire programs Friday and Saturday evenings for visitors staying at the Bandy Creek Campground and any others who wish to attend. Depending on visitation patterns, the programs may continue into October. The programs range from talks about how to avoid ticks and other safety concerns, through presentations on the American long rifle and other historical topics, to storytelling. These programs are presented at the campfire amphitheater between Loops A and B in the campground or in the larger amphitheater north of the Bandy Creek Visitor Center, or at the visitor center in case of rain. Short

Longhunter Program

talks are also sometimes presented during the day at the visitor center. The schedule for these programs is posted on campground bulletin boards and at the visitor center and is advertised in area newspapers.

At this writing, a campfire program at the Blue Heron Campground awaits construction of an amphitheater or campfire circle where the programs can be held. Short talks are given at the mining community during the time the scenic train operates.

Junior Ranger Program

Designed for 4- to 12-year-olds, the Junior Ranger Program helps children learn about the National Park Service and the BSFNRRA. A child may pick up a handbook at the visitor centers or at the Blue Heron Interpretive Center at the mining community. The fun activities in the handbook include hiking, attending programs, and visiting natural and cultural areas within the park.

After completing the activities in the handbook, each child goes back to the visitor center or Blue Heron and talks with a ranger, who may ask questions to see what the child has learned. The child then receives an official Junior Ranger Badge.

Patch Hike

Groups such as Boy Scouts and Girl Scouts can receive a patch for doing a hike that includes the Oscar Blevins and John Litton Farm Loops and completing activities along the way. You may pick up the leader's guide and hiking guides for each member at the Bandy Creek Visitor Center; these guides are also available to the general public. The leader's guide includes a form to be sent to the Great Smoky Mountains Council of the Boy Scouts in order to receive the patches.

Special Events

Pioneer encampment

Throughout the year, the park sponsors special events for the general visitor and for those participating in specialized outdoor activities. For the general visitor, the events might be pioneer encampments where volunteers demonstrate and explain the lifestyles and skills of the early pioneers. Or you can participate in the Haunting in the Hills Storytelling Festival in September. A number of special activities and programs are conducted in cooperation with the Big South Fork Scenic Railway.

Events for specific outdoor activities include the Big South Fork Competitive Ride held in the spring; horseback riders compete in handling and conditioning of the horse.

Contact the Bandy Creek Visitor Center for a schedule of events and who to contact.

VIP Program

Volunteers in Park (VIP) is a way for groups and individuals to donate their time and skills in support of the BSFNRRA and its resources. The VIP Program has been instituted in just about every park in the National Park System. At the Big South Fork, individuals can work at the visitor centers, do trail maintenance, adopt an area to monitor and maintain, present demonstrations and prepare special events, answer mail requests, give guided nature walks, help in producing inventories, and serve as campground hosts. VIPs may work a few hours a week or month, seasonally or full-time. To be a VIP, you must complete an application that asks about your talents, skills, and interests. Some interesting projects could include working in historical restoration and historical research if you have the required skills.

Partners in Parks/Partners in Education

Partners in Parks and Partners in Education is a way for schools, businesses, and other groups to donate time and resources to support the park. Schools may work on educational projects, especially materials for interpretation. Businesses may donate materials, sponsor specific projects like the printing of brochures, and even donate the time of their employees to work in the park.

Under this program, the 1991 biology classes of Scott County High School assisted in the development of the self-guided tree-identification walk along the Angel Falls Trail and the accompanying brochure.

Big South Fork Trail Riders Association

This association of horseback riders supports trail riding in the park by raising money for trail maintenance and participating in trail cleanup. Among their contributions was the donation of a horse to the park for rangers to use in patrolling the horse trails.

Big South Fork Saddle Club

Members of this club have been riding the trails in the Big South Fork area for over 25 years. The club provides information and recommendations on the horse trails in the park; you can contact them at the address listed in the back. The club holds horse shows at Winfield Park in Winfield, TN, on US27; members also participate in the cleanup of trails and access roads.

Friends of the Big South Fork

This Friends group of volunteers is dedicated to improving visitors' understanding of the Big South Fork area. They assist by raising funds for the recreation area and providing volunteers for needed projects. To join or to volunteer, contact the Friends at the address in Appendix A.

Tennessee Citizens for Wilderness Planning

TCWP is a Tennessee conservation organization that was instrumental in the establishment of the BSFNRRA by bringing attention to the scenic values of the area, lobbying for support in establishing a park, and assisting with studies and writing legislation. In addition to being involved in various other state and national conservation issues, the organization continues to work for the preservation of the Big South Fork, ensuring that the authorized legislation is adequately and wisely implemented and helping to see that the park receives adequate federal funding for land acquisition and operating expenses.

Part III
Other Opportunities Nearby

Communities and Parks Surrounding the Big South Fork

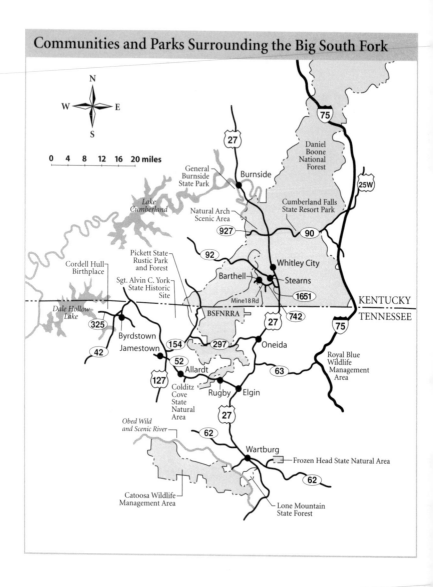

Surrounding Communities

Communities surrounding the BSFNRRA offer accommodations and a touch of history. You'll find the descendants of the people of the Big South Fork and more recent arrivals ready to welcome visitors.

Oneida, Tennessee

Oneida was originally part of the community of Pine Creek. Then in the 1870s the Southern Railroad was built through the area, connecting Cincinnati, Ohio, with Chattanooga. A more populated community grew up near the rail line, and when a post office was established, the community was named for Oneida, New York; some of the investors in the railroad and community were from there and recognized the similarity of the area's rolling hills and stands of white pine.

Located at the junction of US27 and TN297, Oneida still supports lumbering and wood products industries. Just north of the junction, the headquarters of the old O&W Railroad still stands on the west side of US27, an elegant two-story brick building that now houses a chiropractic clinic; the Oneida O&W depot was located across the street where the First National Bank now stands. Contact the Scott County Chamber of Commerce for details on the motels and restaurants in Oneida and the surrounding communities.

For accommodations near the national river and recreation area, Big South Fork Wilderness Resorts has rental cabins on Station Camp Road, just before the park boundary. They also have rental cabins on the west side of the park off TN297 and near the Bear Creek Scenic Area in Kentucky.

Jamestown, Tennessee

Located on the west side of the park, Jamestown was once the home of John Marshall Clemens, the father of Samuel Langhorne Clemens, better known as Mark Twain. It is said that Mark Twain was conceived in Jamestown, but the family moved to Missouri before he was born. You'll see references to

O&W Depot at Jamestown

Mark Twain in some of the signs in the area. A small park near the center of town protects a small spring from which the Clemens family got their water while living nearby.

North of the downtown area on old US127, you'll find the York Institute, founded by Sgt. Alvin C. York, the World War I hero, to educate the children of the region. You can continue north on US127 to York's hometown of Pall Mall. To the south, you can visit Highland Manor Winery and sample their award-winning wines and tour the winery.

Jamestown is located at the junction of US127 and TN52. West of the town center on TN52, at the corner of Depot Lane, the old O&W Railroad depot, a large wooden structure built in 1930, still stands on the south side of the highway. Contact the Fentress County Chamber of Commerce for details on the restaurants and motels in Jamestown and surrounding communities. The Chamber is housed in a historic jail, built in 1898, located in Jamestown on TN52. Some accommodations are available close to the national river and recreation area near the junction of TN297 and TN154; see listings in Appendix A.

Whitley City, Kentucky

Originally the community of Coolidge, the town changed its name in 1912 to Whitley City when McCreary County was formed. It had been part of Whitley County, which was named for Col. William Whitley, a frontiersman who was an early Indian fighter.

Whitley City is located on US27 near the northern end of the BSFNRRA. Contact the McCreary County Tourism Commission for details on the restaurants and motels in Whitley City and surrounding communities.

Rugby, Tennessee

Founded as the last English colony in the United States, Rugby served as a refuge where the second sons of English gentry, who had no inheritance, could earn a living through farming and industry without sullying their families' reputations. The colony had been the idea of English author Thomas Hughes; he helped acquire land and encouraged immigration. The town took the name of the English school Hughes had attended and which was the setting for his famous novel *Tom Brown's School Days*. Rugby was dedicated in 1880.

Kingstone Lisle, the home of Thomas Hughes in historic Rugby

The town took shape as houses were built and a school, church, inn, and library were erected. The colony was never a great financial success. Most of the colonists eventually moved on to other opportunities.

In the 1960s, an association formed, now called "Historic Rugby," that took over the management and preservation of many of the historic structures in the town. You'll find the school, church, library, founder's home, and several of the Victorian homes nestled in the forest of the Cumberland Plateau. Tours of the historic community begin at the visitor center, which is in the old school building. Events and crafts workshops are held year round. You can stay the night at one of several bed-and-breakfasts and have dinner at the local cafe; to the west on TN52, there's the R. M. Brooks General Store and Post Office, a traditional rural store. Contact Historic Rugby (see Appendix A) for details.

Rugby sits on TN52 between Elgin on US27 to the east and Jamestown on US127 to the west. The community borders the BSFNRRA on the south; it's about 35 miles from the Bandy Creek Visitor Center. Near the cemetery in the community, you can walk the Gentlemen's Swimming Hole Trail down to the Clear Fork River within the park.

Allardt, Tennessee

Founded soon after Rugby, Allardt was a German colony established by M. H. Allardt and Bruno Gernt. Allardt died shortly afterward, and the community was named for him. The Allardt colonists were more successful than those at Rugby in establishing an economic base in agriculture, mining, and timbering. But the remaining historic buildings of the present community are less extensive and less elaborate than those at Rugby, and so for that reason perhaps, the community remains less known.

The town lies about 12 miles west of Rugby on TN52. You'll find in the community the Bruno Gernt House, built in 1881–1882 and now a bed-and-breakfast. The Gernt family still manages the family's holdings from the Gernt Office, a small white building near the center of town. In addition

Bruno Gernt House

to the Gernt House, they also have secluded log cabins for rent by the week or weekend. The old Allardt Schoolhouse has also been converted into a bed-and-breakfast.

Stearns, Kentucky

Established in 1902 by Stearns Coal and Lumber, this company town grew up in the virtual wilderness to serve as the central point for the company's operations. The town was founded by William A. Kinne, land and timber agent for the company who lived in Stearns thereafter, and E. E. Barthell, the company's general counsel. The site they chose for the new town was a Southern Railroad siding and crosstie yard, locally called "Hemlock." The Stearns company created in the town the first entirely electric lumber yard in the country. To power the operation, the company constructed a steam power plant fueled by waste from the lumber yard. In another innovative move, the steam from the power plant boilers was used to heat the of-

Stearns in 1919
(Courtesy of Stearns Museum)

fices, businesses, and executive residences, and the resulting distilled water filled the town's water system. With divestiture that began in later years, Stearns was no longer a company town by 1977.

Stearns sits at the junction of KY92 and KY1651 west of US27. The Big South Fork Kentucky Visitor Center is just to the east of town on KY92.

The McCreary County Museum in Stearns is housed in the old company headquarters on the hill; the 1907 building also contained the town's bank. You'll find in the museum exhibits, old photos, and artifacts about the Stearns Company and other local history; the artifacts include the drill bit from the first commercial oil well, which was located on Martin Beaty's land now within the BSFNRRA. There's a small charge to tour the museum, which is open most days except Mondays during the spring, summer, and fall, but is closed late fall and winter.

In the middle of the town area stands a complex of buildings, completed in the 1920s, that once contained Stores No. 1 and No. 3 for groceries and hardware, plus the dentist's and doctor's offices. A restaurant still occupies the old coffee shop. The theater or opera house is now a craft and gift shop.

Just to the northwest of the museum was the hotel that was burned in 1908 to dislodge union organizers who had taken refuge there for fear of being arrested. The hotel was rebuilt after the fire but in later years was torn down. To the east once stood the community hall.

Up the hill behind the McCreary County Museum, on the continuation of KY1651, you'll find the neighborhoods and houses where the company officials lived. Many of the wood frame houses date from 1910. The last Stearns family home is the large white house behind the museum.

In the community you'll also find a golf course, one of the oldest in Kentucky. There are a few places to stay; check with the McCreary County Tourism Commission for lodgings in the area.

The R. L. Stearns Wholesale Grocery warehouse stretches along the railroad tracks on the east side of town. Robert L. Stearns, the son of company founder Justus Stearns, took over company operations from his father; he had lived in Stearns in the early years and returned for a few months of each year thereafter. His son, Robert L. Stearns Jr., was a later president of the company and lived in Stearns most of his adult life.

The warehouse has been restored and is now the depot for the Big South Fork Scenic Railway that provides

Big South Fork Scenic Railway
(Courtesy of Lavidge & Associates, Inc.)

train rides into the Big South Fork Gorge to the Blue Heron Mining Community. The scenic train ride following the route of the K&T Railroad along Roaring Paunch Creek is about 40 minutes one-way; the entire trip with layover at Blue Heron runs about 3 hours. There is also a stop at the Barthell Mining Camp. The train operates most days April through October; inquire about the current schedule and the fare.

Barthell, Kentucky

Barthell was the first coal mining camp along the Kentucky & Tennessee Railroad. The camp was named for E. E. Barthell, the Stearns Coal and Lumber Company's general counsel who helped found Stearns, Kentucky. The first coal mined by the Stearns Company and shipped out of the watershed on the K&T came from Mine #1 at Barthell on June 1, 1903. The land for the community and the coal operations was originally leased by the Stearns Company but was eventually purchased in 1923. The small community once had a population of 300, consisting mainly of families. In addition to houses, the town included Stearns' Store No. 2, which included the post office. A schoolhouse that held classes nine months out of the year doubled as the church. The tipple at Barthell burned in 1943, and the coal from that camp's mines was thereafter hauled to the Blue Heron Tipple.

As the coal camp was abandoned due to the slowdown in the industry, the community's structures were dismantled by the company during the period 1952–62, and the town disappeared except for a few foundations. But in recent years, the community has been reconstructed by the local Koger family; the buildings include the company store, the motor house with displays of mining equipment, the school, the bath house, the barber shop, and doctor's office. Several cabins have been built resembling the homes of the mining families and are available for overnight stays. A walking tour of the community passes by old mine openings in the gorge wall above the camp.

Barthell Coal Camp

In addition to riding the scenic railway to Barthell, you can also drive to the community. Take the Mine 18 Road down toward Blue Heron, and at 3 miles from the Bear Creek Scenic Area turnoff, or about 2 miles before Blue Heron, turn on a gravel road to the right that leads to the community. There is a fee for touring the reconstructed Barthell.

Parks and Preserves

Although the BSFNRRA is the focus for outdoor activities in this part of the region, the surrounding area has a number of other parks and preserves where you can find additional opportunities for outdoor recreation.

Pickett State Rustic Park and Forest

Adjacent to the BSFNRRA on the western edge of the park in Tennessee, Pickett State Rustic Park and Forest possesses a similar geology. You'll find stone arches and rock shelters throughout the park. Sandstone bluffs along Thompson Creek form a small canyon as the water flows to meet Rock Creek and eventually joins the Big South Fork in Kentucky.

To get to the park, take TN297 west from the Bandy Creek Visitor Center to its junction with TN154. Turn north for 2.7 miles to the park entrance; you'll pass the road on the right into the Middle Creek area before the entrance.

There is no lodge in the park, but it does have chalets and cottages for rent year-round. The park's campground has forty sites, and there's also a group camp with bathhouses, bunkhouses, cabins, and a kitchen/dining lodge. Activities include picnicking, hiking the numerous trails, and swimming, boating, and fishing on the small lake created by the Thompson Creek Dam.

Sgt. Alvin C. York State Historic Site

This Tennessee state historic site commemorates Sgt. Alvin C. York. During a World War I battle in the Argonne Forest of France, he single-handedly captured 132 German soldiers, killed 28, and so neutralized several machine-gun bunkers, thereby protecting a railroad, for which he was awarded the Congressional Medal of Honor. A movie was later made of his exploits.

After returning to his home in Pall Mall, Tennessee, York operated the mill you can visit today. The historic site also includes the old York homeplace, a store and post office once owned by York, a bible school he built, and his burial site.

Sergeant York Grist Mill

To get to Pall Mall, head south on TN154 from the intersection with TN297. In 10 miles turn north on US127 and travel another 9 miles to the community.

Dale Hollow Lake and Cordell Hull Birthplace

If you're interested in lake boating and fishing, you can make your way to Dale Hollow Lake on the Obey River tributary of the Cumberland River west of the park. Continue on US127 north from Pall Mall for another 8 miles, turn west on TN42, and watch for several exits for lake access in the vicinity of Byrdstown. While you're in the area, you can also stop by the Cordell Hull Birthplace, a historic site on TN325, Cordell Hull Memorial Drive, west off TN42. As secretary of state, Hull authored the U.S. "Good Neighbor" policy and laid the groundwork for the founding of the United Nations, for which he received the Nobel Peace Prize.

Daniel Boone National Forest

Surrounding the northern part of the BSFNRRA in Kentucky, Daniel Boone National Forest offers more opportunity for outdoor recreation. Hunting, fishing, four-wheel driving, hiking, horseback riding, camping, and backpacking are approved activities. The Sheltowee Trace National Recreation Trail travels south 257 miles through the national forest to enter the BSFNRRA and end at Pickett State Rustic Park and Forest on the west. Off KY1363 west of the park, the national forest has the Bell Farm Horse Camp with campsites but no water or electricity. From the west end of KY1363, following the graveled FSR564 and then turning south on FSR137, you'll find the Hemlock Grove Picnic Area and the Great Meadows Campground with campsites, drinking water, and pit toilets but no hookups. Farther down FSR137, the Rock Creek Trailhead gives access to the John Muir Trail, the Sheltowee Trace, and the Forest Service's Parkers Mountain Trail. The national forest's Barren Fork Horse Camp is located behind the Stearns Ranger District Office north of Whitley City on US27; several horse trails lead out from the camp.

Cumberland Falls State Resort Park

Surrounded by Daniel Boone National Forest, Cumberland Falls State Resort Park lies north of the BSFNRRA. Head north on US27 to a right turn on KY90 that leads to the Kentucky state park, about a 20-mile drive north from Whitley City.

Cumberland Falls on the Cumberland River is the park's main attraction. This broad waterfall is sometimes called the "Niagara of the South." On clear, full-moon nights with plenty of water coming over the falls, you can see a moonbow—a rainbow that appears in the mist of the falls. It's sometimes

Cumberland Falls

claimed that this is the only moonbow in the Western Hemisphere, but in fact there are several others, such as at Niagara Falls and Yosemite Falls. The park has a lodge, cabins, duplexes, tennis courts, a swimming pool, and a campground with water and electric hookups.

Natural Arch Scenic Area

On the way to Cumberland Falls, you can stop off at the national forest's Natural Arch Scenic Area to see one of the large natural sandstone arches found on the Cumberland Plateau. Just before the right turn on KY90, turn left on KY927 and drive to the entrance on the right in 2 miles. You'll find picnicking and hiking trails that lead to the massive arch with a span of 100 feet and a clearance of 60 feet.

Natural Arch

General Burnside State Park and Lake Cumberland

The most significant Civil War event in the Big South Fork region occurred when President Lincoln ordered General Ambrose Burnside to invade East Tennessee from Kentucky. Rather than attempting a pass through Cumberland Gap, which was held by the Confederates at the time, Burnside marched his troops through the Big South Fork country. Burnside, Kentucky, and General Burnside State Park are named in his honor.

Twenty miles north of Whitley City on US27, you'll find a causeway that leads to the island park located where the Big South Fork joins the Cumberland River. This recreation park has a swimming pool, golf course, and a campground with 110 sites for tents and trailers; there are electric and water hookups. You can use the park as a base from which to fish and explore the waters of Lake Cumberland.

Colditz Cove State Natural Area

This 75-acre Tennessee state natural area contains 60-foot-high Northrup Falls set in a cove of hemlock and rhododendron. A mile-long loop trail drops into a small gorge and takes you behind the waterfall. Rudolph and Arnold Colditz donated the land for the natural area to the state. The waterfall is named for a family that once lived at the head of the falls. The trail was constructed by the Cumberland Chapter of the Tennessee Trails Association.

Eleven miles west of Rugby on TN52, just inside the town limits of Allardt, turn south on the Crooked Creek Road and drive one mile to parking and the trailhead on the right.

Northrup Falls at Colditz Cove State Natural Area

Obed Wild and Scenic River

To the south, the Obed River carves a deep gorge in the surface of the Cumberland Plateau, creating a similar topography to the Big South Fork Gorge. Designated a national wild and scenic river in 1976, the river has become known as one of the best whitewater rivers in the southeast. Paddlers value the wilderness experience along the isolated 45 miles of the river corridor, including stretches along the tributaries, Clear Creek and Daddys Creek. The difficulty ranges from II to V and so the runs are for experienced paddlers only. There is a picnic area and campground (no hookups) at Nemo Bridge on the Emory River near the Obed's junction with the Emory.

The wild and scenic river is managed under the direction of the BSFNRRA superintendent. The visitor center is located in the town of Wartburg, which was originally a German colony founded in 1848. Take US27 south from Oneida. Wartburg is about 50 miles from the BSFNRRA Bandy Creek Visitor Center.

The Obed passes through the Catoosa Wildlife Management Area, an 80,000-acre preserve managed by the Tennessee Wildlife Resources Agency. Hunting and fishing are popular activities. The Obed River Gorge also offers plenty of opportunity for climbing and rappelling; hiking trails are being constructed.

Obed Wild and Scenic River

Frozen Head State Natural Area

Near the Obed Wild and Scenic River, Frozen Head State Natural Area provides more opportunity for hiking and backpacking in its 11,869 acres that includes Frozen Head Mountain. From Wartburg, take TN62 southeast 4 miles

Emory Gap Falls at Frozen Head State Natural Area

to a turn north on a paved road that leads 2 miles to the natural area. About 50 miles of trails wander through the park. There's also picnicking and tent camping. Register at the visitor center for overnight camping in the backcountry.

Lone Mountain State Forest

This Tennessee state forest offers hiking, horseback riding, and hunting among its outdoor activities. Located in the vicinity of Frozen Head State Park and the Obed Wild and Scenic River, Lone Mountain State Forest lies to the west of US27; 4 miles southeast of Wartburg, turn right on Clayton Howard Road to enter the forest.

Royal Blue Wildlife Management Area

This Tennessee WMA is accessible at the TN63 exit off I-75. The area lies east of I-75 and west along TN63 as you head for the BSFNRRA from the interstate. Managed by the Tennessee Wildlife Resources Agency, this preserve shelters an open hardwood forest that lies on the eastern edge of the Cumberland Plateau; a reclamation project will rehabilitate abandoned strip mines in the area. Activities here include hunting, fishing, hiking, mountain biking, horseback riding, and four-wheel and ATV driving. Motorized vehicles, horses, and bicycles must use only existing roads. A special ATV area is planned, and camping will be allowed in designated camping areas.

Appendix A: Addresses, Telephone Numbers, and Websites

Big South Fork National River and Recreation Area
4564 Leatherwood Road
Oneida, TN 37841
www.nps.gov/biso
423/569-9778 (Park Headquarters)
931/879-3625 (Bandy Creek Visitor Center)
931/879-4869 (Bandy Creek Campground and Group Camps)
606/376-5073 (Kentucky Visitor Center)
606/376-3787 (Blue Heron Mining Community)
800/365-2267 or *http://reservations.nps.gov* (camping reservations)
http://water.usgs.gov/realtime.html (flow readings)

Accommodations and Restaurants

Allardt Schoolhouse Bed &
Breakfast
P.O. Box 115
Allardt, TN 38504
931/879-6560 or 931/879-8056

Bacara's Family Restaurant
329 Wheeler Lane
Jamestown, TN 38556
931/879-7121

Big South Fork Motor Lodge
HC 69, Box 335
Stearns, KY 42647
606/376-3156

Big South Fork Wilderness Resorts
1463 Big Ridge Road
Oneida, TN 37841
423/569-9847

Bruno Gernt House
East Fork Stables
P.O. Box 156
Allardt, TN 38504
800/978-7245

Charit Creek Lodge
250 Apple Valley Road
Sevierville, TN 37862
423/429-5704

Clear Fork Farm Bed & Breakfast
328 Shirley Ford Road
Robbins, TN 37852
423/628-2967

Grey Gables Bed & Breakfast
P.O. Box 5252, Hwy. 52
Rugby, TN 37733
423/628-5252

Laurel Creek Travel Park
150 Laurel Creek Road
Jamestown, TN 38556
931/879-7696

Marcum-Porter House
P.O. Box 369
Stearns, KY 42647
606/376-2242

Newbury House, Percy Cottage,
and Pioneer Cottage
c/o Historic Rugby
P.O. Box 8
Rugby, TN 37733
Reservations: 423/628-2449

Wildwood Lodge Bed & Breakfast
3636 Pickett Park Hwy.
Jamestown, TN 38556
931/879-9454

Activities and Attractions

Big South Fork Scenic Railway
P.O. Box 368
Stearns, KY 42647
800/462-5664
www.bsfsry.com

Cordell Hull Birthplace and
Museum State Historic Site
1300 Cordell Hull Memorial Drive
Byrdstown, TN 38549
931/864-3247

Cumberland Falls State Resort Park
7351 Hwy. 90
Corbin, KY 40701
606/528-4121
Reservations: 800/325-0063

Frozen Head State Natural Area
964 Flat Fork Road
Wartburg, TN 37887
423/346-3318

General Burnside State Park
P.O. Box 488
Burnside, KY 42519
606/561-4104

Historic Rugby
P.O. Box 8
Rugby, TN 37733
423/628-2430
www.historicrugby.org

Koger-Barthell Mining Town
P.O. Box 53
Whitley City, KY 42653
800/550-5748

McCreary County Museum
P.O. Box 452
Stearns, KY 42647
606/376-5730

Obed Wild and Scenic River
P.O. Box 429
Wartburg, TN 37887
423/346-6295
www.nps.gov/obed

Pickett State Rustic Park and
Forest
Rock Creek Route, Box 174
Jamestown, TN 38556
931/879-5821

Sgt. Alvin C. York State Historic Site
General Delivery
Pall Mall, TN 38577
931/879-4026

Emergency Services

Fentress County Ambulance
931/879-8147

Fentress County General Hospital
W. Central Avenue
Jamestown, TN
931/879-8171

Fentress County Sheriff
Jamestown, TN
931/879-8142

McCreary County Ambulance
606/376-5062

McCreary County Sheriff
606/376-2322

Scott County Ambulance
423/569-6000

Scott County Hospital
Hwy US27
Oneida, TN
423/569-8521

Scott County Sheriff
Huntsville, TN
423/663-2245

Organizations and Government Agencies

Big South Fork Saddle Club
4099 Helenwood Detour Road
Oneida, TN 37841

Big South Fork Trail Riders
Association
760 Firetower Road
Robbins, TN 37852

Fentress County Chamber of
Commerce
P.O. Box 1294
Jamestown, TN 38556
931/879-9948
www.jamestowntn.org

Friends of the Big South Fork
P.O. Box 5407
Oneida, TN 37841
423/569-1599

Kentucky Department of Fish
and Wildlife Resources
#1 Game Farm Road
Frankfort, KY 40601
502/564-4336

McCreary County Tourism
Commission
P.O. Box 72
Whitley City, KY 42653
606/376-3008

North American Trail Ride
Conference (NATRC)
P.O. Box 2136
Ranchos de Taos, NM 87557-2136
505/751-4198
www.natrc.org

Scott County Chamber of
Commerce
P.O. Box 4442
Oneida, TN 37841
800/645-6905
www.scottcounty.com

Stearns Ranger District
Daniel Boone National Forest
P.O. Box 429
Whitley City, KY 42653
606/376-5323

Tennessee Citizens for
Wilderness Planning
130 Tabor Road
Oak Ridge, TN 37830
www.korrnet.org/tcwp

Tennessee Wildlife Resources
Agency
464 Industrial Blvd.
Crossville, TN 38555
800/262-6704

Horse Camps, Stables, and Other Services

Bandy Creek Stables
1845 Old Sunbright Road
Jamestown, TN 38556
931/879-4013

Big South Fork Horse Camps
P.O. Box 4411
Oneida, TN 37841
423/569-3321

Sheltowee Trace Outfitters
P.O. Box 1060
Whitley City, KY 42653
800/541-RAFT

Southeast Pack Trips, Inc.
299 Dewey Burk Road
Jamestown, TN 38556
931/879-2260

Tally Ho Stables
P.O. Box 4773
Oneida, TN 37841
423/569-9472

Appendix B:
Plant Life of the Big South Fork

Trees

Starred species (*) are rare, threatened, endangered, or of special concern.

Broad-leafed

Alder
Allegheny Chinquapin*
American Beech
American Holly
Ashes
    Green Ash
    White Ash
Basswood
Big Tooth Aspen
Birches
    River Birch
    Yellow Birch
Blackgum
Black Locust
Black Walnut
Boxelder
Buckeye
Butternut*
Chestnut
Cottonwood
Dogwoods
    Swamp Dogwood
    Flowering Dogwood
Elms
    American Elm
    Red Elm
    Winged Elm
Fringetree
Hackberry
Hazelnut

Hickories
    Bitternut Hickory
    Mockernut Hickory
    Pignut Hickory
    Shagbark Hickory
Hophornbeam
Ironwood
Magnolias
    Bigleaf Magnolia
    Cucumber Magnolia
    Fraser Magnolia
    Umbrella Magnolia
Maples
    Red Maple
    Striped Maple
    Sugar Maple
Oaks
    Black Oak
    Blackjack Oak
    Chestnut Oak
    Northern Red Oak
    Post Oak
    Scarlet Oak
    Southern Red Oak
    White Oak
Pawpaw
Persimmon
Redbud
Red Mulberry
Sassafras

Serviceberry
Sourwood
Sweetgum
Sycamore
Tulip Poplar
Willow
    Black Willow
    Silky Willow
Witchhazel

Conifers

Cedars
    Northern White Cedar*
    Red Cedar
Eastern Hemlock
Pines
    Eastern White Pine
    Pitch Pine
    Shortleaf Pine
    Virginia Pine

Fall Color

Reds

Dogwood
Oaks
    Northern Red Oak
    Southern Red Oak
    White Oak
Red Maple
Serviceberry

Scarlets

Blackgum
Scarlet Oak
Sourwood
Sumac
Sweetgum

Yellows

American Beech
Basswood

Birch
    River Birch
    Yellow Birch
Black Walnut
Buckeye
Chestnut Oak
Cottonwood
Hickory
Hophornbeam
Pawpaw
Persimmon
Poplar
Redbud
Red Mulberry
Striped Maple

Red-Oranges

Sassafras
Sugar Maple

Wildflowers

Starred species (*) are rare, threatened, endangered, or of special concern.

Early Spring (March)

Bloodroot
Early Saxifrage
Harbinger-of-Spring
Hepatica
Purple Cress
Purslane Speedwell
Rue Anemone
Spring Beauty
Star Chickweed
Trout Lily
Twinleaf

Stone Crop
Violets
    Birdfoot Violet
    Common Blue Violet
    Halberd-leaved Violet
    Long-spurred Violet
    Smooth Yellow Violet
Trilliums
    Erect Trillium
    Large-flowered Trillium
    Yellow Trillium
Winter Cress

Mid-Spring (April)

Allegheny Spurge
Blue Cohosh
Blue Phlox
Bluets
Buttercups
Common Cinquefoil
Crested Dwarf Iris
Cut-leaved Toothwort
Dutchman's Breeches
Dwarf Larkspur
Fire Pink
Foamflower
Golden Ragwort
Little Brown Jug
Mercury Spurge*
Mountain Spurge
Pennywort
Pussy Toes
Slender Toothwort
Spiderwort
Spring Cress
Squirrel Corn

Late Spring (May)

Bindweed
Chickweed
Coreopsis
Dwarf Dandelion
Dwarf Ginseng*
False Solomon's-Seal
Green and Gold*
Indian Cucumber-Root
Indian Pink
Jack-in-the-Pulpit
Lady's Slippers
    Pink Lady's Slipper*
    Yellow Lady's Slipper*
Large-flowered Bellwort
Lyre-leaved Sage
May Apple
Mountain Laurel
Queen Anne's Lace
Sandworts
    Appalachian Sandwort*
    Cumberland Sandwort*

Showy Orchis
Solomon's-Seal
Sweet Cicely
Trailing Arbutus
Violets
    Canada Violet
    Swamp White Violet
    Sweet White Violet
    White Violet
Violet Wood Sorrel
Virginia Bluebells
White Baneberry
Wild Columbine
Wild Geranium
Wild Oats
Wild Sweet William
Wild Yam
Wood Nettle
Yellowroot

Early Summer (June)

Alum-Root
Beard-Tongue
Black Cohosh
Blue-eyed Grass
Butterflyweed
Common Milkweed
Common Skullcap
Daisy Fleabane
Evening Primrose
Flame Azalea
Goat's-Beard
Goat's-Rue
Hawkweeds
    Orange Hawkweed
    Rough Hawkweed*
Hop Clover
Indian Pipe
Lamb's Quarters
Lizard's Tail
Meadow Parsnip

Ox-eye Daisy
Pipsissewa (Spotted Winter-
    green)
Putty-Root
Ragwort
Rhododendrons
    Catawba Rhododendron
    Rosebay Rhododendron
Ruellia
St. Johnswort
Teaberry (Wintergreen)
Venus' Looking Glass
Viper's Bugloss
Waterleaf
Whorled Loosestrife
Wood-Sage
Yellow Wood Sorrel

Mid-Summer (July)

Agrimony
Bedstraw
Black-eyed Susan
Cardinal Flower
Dodder
Enchanter's Nightshade
False Foxgloves
    Blue Ridge False Foxglove*
    Spreading False Foxglove*
Flowering Spurge
Fringed Loosestrife
Hoary Mountain Mint
Jewelweed
Leatherleaf Meadow Rue*
Nodding Wild Onion
Partridgeberry
Rattlesnake Plantain
Rose Pink
Rosebud Orchis
Sensitive Brier
Smartweed
Spotted Joe-Pye Weed

Tick Trefoil
Virginia Dayflower
White Avens
Wild Hydrangea
Wood Lily*

Late Summer (August)

Asters
    Golden Aster
    New England Aster
    White-topped Aster
Beebalm
Beggarticks
Bergamot
Blazing Star
Blue Monkshood*
Common Thistle
False Foxglove
Great Blue Lobelia
Harebell
Hog Peanut
Horse-Balm
Ironweed
Jerusalem Artichoke
Monkey Flower
Orchids
    Crane-fly Orchid
    Crested Fringed Orchid*
Small Sundrops*
Star Tickseed*

Sunflowers
    Rough-leaved Sunflower
    Woodland Sunflower
Sweet Everlasting
Thread-leaf Sundrops*
Tickseed
Turtlehead
White Lettuce
Yellow Leaf-Cup

Autumn (September–October)

Asters
    Calico Aster
    Eastern Silvery Aster*
    Frost-weed Aster
    Heart-leaved Aster
    Rockcastle Aster*
    White Wood Aster
Autumn Sneezeweed
Gall-of-the-Earth
Goldenrod
Lion's-Foot
Mistflower
Purple Gerardia
Snakeroot
    Lucy Braun's White Snake-
        root*
    White Snakeroot
Sticky Goldenrod*

A Sampling of Other Seed Plants

Starred species (*) are rare, threatened, endangered, or of special concern. Double-starred species (**) are non-native.

Ageratum**
American Barberry*
American Water-Pennywort*
Arrow Arum

Arrow-Wood
Bachelor's Button**
Barren Strawberry
Bastard-Toadflax

Beakrush
Beech-Drops
Beggar Lice
Birthwort
Blue Haw
Boneset
Box Huckleberry
Buckthorn
Buffalo Nut
Bugbane
Bulrush
Bur-Reed
Burdock**
Butternut*
Buttonbush
Carolina Rose
Catbrier
Cattail
Chickory**
Climbing Hydrangea
Clovers
Cocklebur**
Columbo
Common Daisy**
Common Mullein**
Common Rush
Coral Honeysuckle**
Coralberry
Croton
Cumberland Rosemary*
Daffodil**
Dame's Rocket**
Dandelion**
Daylily**
Devil's Walking Stick
Dewberry
Dock**
Dog Fennel**
Duckweed**
Dutchman's Pipe
Elderberry
Elephant's Foot

False Indigo
False Nettle
Fetterbush
Fireweed
Five-Fingers
Fly Poison
Fringed Nutrush*
Frost Grape
Galingale
Golden Alexander
Golden Club*
Golden Seal*
Grasses
    Barley
    Beardgrass*
    Bent Grass
    Big Bluestem
    Bluegrass
    Bottlebrush Grass
    Brome Grass
    Broomsedge
    Cane
    Crabgrass**
    Cut Grass
    Fescue
    Goose Grass**
    Hair Grass
    Indiangrass
    Little Bluestem
    Manna Grass
    Melic Grass
    Needle Grass
    Oat Grass
    Orchard Grass**
    Panic Grass
    Rye Grass**
    Sweet Vernal Grass**
    Switchgrass
    Timothy**
    Velvet Grass**
    Wild Rye Grass
Hairy Snoutbean*

Hardhack
Hawthorn
Hedge Hyssop*
Henbit**
Heronsbill**
Honewort
Honey Locust
Horseweed
Indian Hemp
Indian-Physic
Indian Plantain
Indian Strawberry**
Japanese Honeysuckle**
Jumpseed
Kidneyleaf Grass-of-Parnassus*
Kudzu**
Large-flowered Barbara's Buttons*
Leatherwood
Lespedeza
Leucothoe
Liverleaf
Lopseed
Lousewort
Lovage
Maleberry
Maple-leafed Viburnum
Mexican Tea**
Milkweed
Mimosa**
Mistletoe
Mock Orange*
Morning-Glory
Mountain Camellia
Mountain Witch-Alder*
Muscadine
Nannyberry
New Jersey Tea
Ninebark
Nuttall's Small Reedgrass*
Obedient Plant
Passion Flower
Path Rush

Pepper-Vine
Peppergrass**
Periwinkle**
Pigweed**
Pinweed
Pirate Bush*
Poison Hemlock**
Poison Ivy
Poke Weed
Pondweeds
Possum Haw
Purple Coneflower
Rabbit Foot Clover**
Ragweed**
Riverweeds
Round-leaf Bitter Cress*
Round-leaf Fameflower*
Sedges
    Cypress-swamp Sedge*
    Heavy Sedge*
    Hop Sedge
    Tussock Sedge*
Shortleaf Sneezeweed*
Southern Crabapple*
Southern Heartleaf*
Sparkleberry
Spicebush
Spikerush
Squaw Huckleberry
Squaw-Root
Strawberry Bush
Sumacs
    Fragrant Sumac
    Smooth Sumac
    Winged Sumac
Summer Grape
Swamp Honeysuckle
Swamp Rose
Sweet-Clover**
Sweet Pinesap*
Sweet-Shrub*
Teasle**

Tennessee Pondweed*
Thoroughwort
Threadfoot*
Three-seeded Mercury
Trumpet Creeper
Valerian
Verbena
Vetch
Virginia Creeper
Virginia Heartleaf*
Virginia Spiraea*
Virginia Willow
Wafer-ash
Wapato
Water Hemlock
Water Plantain

Water Willow
Waxweed
White-leaved Leather-Flower*
Whitlow-Grass
Wild Asparagus**
Wild Blackberry
Wild Chervil
Wild Lettuce
Wild Parsnip
Wild Plum
Wild Quinine
Wild Sensitive Plant
Windflower
Woodrush
Yarrow**
Yellow-eyed Grass

Ferns and Related Plants

Starred species (*) are rare, threatened, endangered, or of special concern.

Clubmosses
    Fir Clubmoss
    Ground Cedar
    Ground Pine
    Rock Clubmoss
    Running Pine
    Shining Clubmoss
Ferns
    American Climbing Fern
    Blunt-lobed Woodsia
    Bracken Fern
    Broad Beechfern
    Christmas Fern
    Cinnamon Fern
    Fancy Fern
    Filmy Fern*
    Glade Fern
    Goldie's Woodfern
    Hay-scented Fern

Maidenhair Fern
Marginal Shield Fern
Marsh Fern
New York Fern
Purple Cliffbrake
Resurrection Fern
Rock Cap Fern
Royal Fern
Sensitive Fern
Southern Lady Fern
Spreading Bladder Fern
Sweet Fern*
Wooly-lip Fern
Grapeferns
    Alabama Grapefern
    Common Grapefern
    Rattlesnake Fern
    Southern Adder's-Tongue
    Southern Grapefern

Meadow Spikemoss
Quillwort
Scouring Rush
Spleenworts
    Ebony Spleenwort

Maidenhair Spleenwort
Mountain Spleenwort
Silvery Spleenwort
Walking Fern

Appendix C: Animal Life of the Big South Fork

Mammals

Starred species (*) are rare, threatened, endangered, or of special concern.

Bats
- Big Brown Bat
- Eastern Pipistrel
- Eastern Small-footed Bat*
- Evening Bat
- Gray Bat*
- Hoary Bat
- Indiana Bat*
- Keen's Bat
- Little Brown Bat
- Northern Long-eared Bat*
- Rafinesque's Big-eared Bat*
- Red Bat
- Silver-haired Bat
- Southeastern Bat

Beaver

Black Bear*

Bobcat

Coyote

Eastern Chipmunk

Eastern Cottontail

Foxes
- Gray Fox
- Red Fox

Long-tail Weasel

Meadow Vole

Mice
- Cotton Mouse
- Deer Mouse
- Eastern Harvest Mouse
- Golden Mouse
- House Mouse
- Meadow Jumping Mouse
- White-footed Mouse
- Woodland Jumping Mouse*

Mink

Moles
- Eastern Mole
- Hairy-tail Mole

Muskrat

Raccoon

Rats
- Black Rat
- Eastern Woodrat*
- Hispid Cotton Rat
- Marsh Rice Rat

River Otter*

Shrews
- Least Shrew
- Masked Shrew
- Short-tail Shrew
- Smokey Shrew
- Southeastern Shrew
- Water Shrew

Skunks
- Eastern Spotted Skunk
- Striped Skunk

Squirrels
- Fox Squirrel
- Gray Squirrel
- Southern Flying Squirrel

Virginia Opossum   Wild Pig
White-tailed Deer   Woodchuck

Resident and Migratory Birds

Not all species have been observed, but they are likely to be present.
Starred species (*) are rare, threatened, endangered, or of special concern.

Permanent Residents

American Goldfinch
American Kestrel
American Robin
American Woodcock
Belted Kingfisher
Blue Jay
Brown Thrasher
Brown-headed Cowbird
Canada Goose
Carolina Chickadee
Carolina Wren
Cedar Waxwing
Common Crow
Common Grackle
Doves
    Mourning Dove
    Rock Dove
Eastern Bluebird
Eastern Meadowlark
Eastern Phoebe
European Starling
Great Blue Heron
Hawks
    Cooper's Hawk*
    Red-shouldered Hawk*
    Red-tailed Hawk
    Sharp-shinned Hawk*
Horned Lark
Killdeer
Mallard

Northern Bobwhite
Northern Flicker
Northern Mockingbird
Owls
    Barred Owl
    Common Barn Owl
    Eastern Screech-Owl
    Great Horned Owl
Northern Cardinal
Pine Warbler
Red Crossbill
Red-winged Blackbird
Ruffed Grouse
Rufous-sided Towhee
Sparrows
    Field Sparrow
    House Sparrow
    Song Sparrow
Tufted Titmouse
Vultures
    Black Vulture*
    Turkey Vulture
White-breasted Nuthatch
Wild Turkey
Woodpeckers
    Downy Woodpecker
    Hairy Woodpecker
    Pileated Woodpecker
    Red-bellied Woodpecker
    Red-headed Woodpecker

Summer Residents (Sp, Su, F)

American Redstart
Blue-gray Gnatcatcher
Broad-winged Hawk
Chimney Swift
Chuck-will's-widow
Common Nighthawk
Common Yellowthroat
Cuckoos
    Black-billed Cuckoo
    Yellow-billed Cuckoo
Eastern Kingbird
Eastern Wood Pewee
Flycatchers
    Acadian Flycatcher
    Willow Flycatcher
Gray Catbird
Herons
    Black-crowned Night-Heron
    Green-backed Heron
    Yellow-crowned Night-
        Heron
House Wren
Indigo Bunting
Louisiana Waterthrush
Northern Parula
Orchard Oriole
Ovenbird
Purple Martin
Ruby-throated Hummingbird
Sparrows
    Chipping Sparrow
    Bachman's Sparrow *
    Grasshopper Sparrow
Swallows
    Barn Swallow
    Northern Rough-winged
        Swallow
Tanagers
    Scarlet Tanager
    Summer Tanager

Vireos
    Red-eyed Vireo
    Solitary Vireo
    White-eyed Vireo
    Yellow-throated Vireo
Warblers
    Black and White Warbler
    Black-throated Green
        Warbler
    Cerulean Warbler
    Chestnut-sided Warbler
    Golden-winged Warbler
    Hooded Warbler
    Kentucky Warbler
    Prairie Warbler
    Prothonotary Warbler
    Swainson's Warbler*
    Worm-eating Warbler
    Yellow Warbler
    Yellow-throated Warbler
Whippoorwill
Wood Duck
Wood Thrush
Yellow-breasted Chat

Winter Residents (F, W, Sp)

American Coot
American Widgeon Bobolink
Brown Creeper
Bufflehead
Canvasback
Common Goldeneye
Common Loon
Common Snipe
Dark-eyed Junco
Ducks
    American Black Duck
    Ring-necked Duck

Eagles
    Bald Eagle*
    Golden Eagle*
Evening Grosbeak
Gadwall
Grebes
    Horned Grebe
    Pied-billed Grebe
Green-winged Teal
Hermit Thrush
Kinglets
    Golden-crowned Kinglet
    Ruby-crowned Kinglet
Lesser Scaup
Mergansers
    Common Merganser
    Hooded Merganser
    Red-breasted Merganser
Northern Pintail
Pine Siskin
Purple Finch
Redhead
Red-breasted Nuthatch
Ring-billed Gull
Rusty Blackbird
Sparrows
    Fox Sparrow
    Savannah Sparrow
    Swamp Sparrow
    Tree Sparrow
    White-crowned Sparrow
    White-throated Sparrow
Winter Wren
Yellow-bellied Sapsucker
Yellow-rumped Warbler

Migrants (Sp, F)

American Bittern
Blue-winged Teal
Bobolink

Flycatchers
    Least Flycatcher
    Olive-sided Flycatcher
Northern Harrier
Northern Oriole
Northern Waterthrush
Osprey *
Peregrine Falcon*
Rose-breasted Grosbeak
Sandhill Crane
Sandpipers
    Least Sandpiper
    Pectoral Sandpiper
    Semi-palmated Sandpiper
    Solitary Sandpiper
    Spotted Sandpiper
Sparrows
    Lincoln's Sparrow
    Vesper Sparrow
Swallows
    Bank Swallow
    Cliff Swallow
    Tree Swallow
Thrushes
    Gray-cheeked Thrush
    Swainson's Thrush
Veery
Vireos
    Philadelphia Vireo
    Warbling Vireo
Warblers
    Bay-breasted Warbler
    Blackburnian Warbler
    Blackpoll Warbler
    Black-throated Blue Warbler
    Blue-winged Warbler
    Canada Warbler
    Cape May Warbler
    Connecticut Warbler
    Magnolia Warbler
    Mourning Warbler

Nashville Warbler
Orange-crowned Warbler
Palm Warbler
Tennessee Warbler
Wilson's Warbler

Wrens
Marsh Wren
Sedge Wren
Yellowlegs
Greater Yellowlegs
Lesser Yellowlegs

Reptiles

Starred species (*) are rare, threatened, endangered, or of special concern.

Lizards
Eastern Slender Glass Lizard
Northern Fence Lizard
Six-lined Racerunner
Skinks
Broad-headed Skink
Five-lined Skink
Ground Skink
Northern Coal Skink
Southeastern Five-lined Skink*
Snakes
Black Kingsnake
Black Rat Snake
Eastern Earth Snake
Eastern Garter Snake
Eastern Hognose Snake
Eastern Milk Snake
Eastern Ribbon Snake
Eastern Worm Snake
Midland Brown Snake
Midwest Worm Snake
Northern Black Racer
Northern Copperhead

Northern Pine Snake
Northern Red-bellied Snake
Northern Ringneck Snake
Northern Scarlet Snake
Northern Water Snake
Queen Snake
Rough Green Snake
Scarlet Kingsnake
Southeastern Crowned
Snake
Timber Rattlesnake
Turtles
Cumberland Turtle
Eastern Box Turtle
Eastern Mud Turtle
Eastern Spiny Softshell
Map Turtle
Midland Painted Turtle
Midland Smooth Softshell
Ouachita Map Turtle
Snapping Turtle
Stinkpot
Stripe-necked Musk Turtle

Amphibians

Starred species (*) are rare, threatened, endangered, or of special concern.

Frogs
    Blanchard's Cricket Frog
    Bullfrog
    Gray Treefrog
    Green Frog
    Mountain Chorus Frog
    Pickerel Frog
    Southern Leopard Frog
    Spring Peeper
    Upland Chorus Frog
    Wood Frog
Salamanders
    Eastern Tiger Salamander
    Four-toed Salamander
    Green Salamander*
    Hellbender*
    Long-tailed Salamander
    Marbled Salamander
    Midland Mud Salamander

Mudpuppy
Northern Dusky Salamander
Northern Red Salamander
Northern Spring Salamander
Northern Two-lined Salamander
Red-spotted Newt
Seal Salamander
Slimy Salamander
Small-mouthed Salamander
Spotted Salamander
Zigzag Salamander
Toads
    American Toad
    Eastern Narrow-mouthed Toad
    Eastern Spadefoot
    Fowler's Toad

Fish

Starred species (*) are rare, threatened, endangered, or of special concern.

Bass
    Coosa Bass
    Kentucky Bass
    Largemouth Bass
    Rock Bass
    Smallmouth Bass
    Spotted Bass
    Striped Bass/Rockfish
    White Bass
Bigeye Chub
Black Redhorse
Bluegill
Brook Silverside

Buffalo
Catfish
    Channel Catfish
    Flathead Catfish
Carp
Crappie
Creek Chub
Daces
    Blacknose Dace
    Rosyside Dace
    Southern Redbelly Dace
Darters
    Arrow Darter

Ashy Darter*
Banded Darter
Barcheek Darter
Blackside Darter
Bluebreast Darter
Channel Darter
Dusky Darter
Duskytail Darter*
Emerald Darter
Greenside Darter
Olive Darter*
Rainbow Darter
Speckled Darter
Spotted Darter
Stripetail Darter
Tippecanoe Darter*
Drum
Gar
Log Perch
Northern Hog Sucker
Ohio Muskellunge
Paddlefish
Quillback Carpsucker
Redhorses
Golden Redhorse
Northern Redhorse
Sauger

Shiners
Common Shiner
Emerald Shiner
Mimic Shiner
Rosefin Shiner
Rosyface Shiner*
Sand Shiner
Sawfin Shiner*
Spotfin Shiner
Telescope Shiner
Tennessee Shiner
Whitetail Shiner
Shovelnose Sturgeon
Slender Madtom
Stonecat
Stoneroller
Sunfish
Green Sunfish
Longear Sunfish
Trout
Brook Trout
Brown Trout
Rainbow Trout
Walleye
Warmouth
White Sucker
Yellow Bullhead

Mussels and Crustaceans

Starred species (*) are rare, threatened, endangered, or of special concern.

Big South Fork Crayfish*
Mussels
Cumberland Bean Pearly
Mussel*
Cumberland Elktoe*
Cumberlandian Combshell*
Fluted Kidneyshell*
Heelsplitter
Kidneyshell

Little-wing Pearly Mussel*
Mucket
Mule Ear
Oyster Mussel*
Pink Lady-Finger
Pistol Grip
Pocketbook
Tan Riffleshell*
Tennessee Clubshell*
White Wartyback

Appendix D:
Selected References

Birdwell, Michael E. *Coal Mining in the Big South Fork Area of Kentucky and Tennessee.* Cookeville, Tenn.: Tennessee Technological University, 1990.

Blevins, Laccie W., and Ray E. Blevins. *Jonathan Blevins Sr. of Virginia and His Descendants.* Johnson City, Tenn.: The Overmountain Press, 1982.

Des Jean, Tom. "Prehistory—Introduction and Conceptual Framework." Unpublished paper, National Park Service, BSFNRRA.

———. "Nineteenth Century Burial Practices of the Upper Cumberland Plateau." Draft manuscript, National Park Service, BSFNRRA.

Fiegel, Kurt H. "Disputing the Titusville Myth." Unpublished paper. Research on the first oil well.

Howell, Benita J. *A Survey of Folklife Along the Big South Fork of the Cumberland River.* Knoxville, Tenn.: The University of Tennessee, 1981.

Humphrey, Steve E. "The History of the No Business and Station Camp Communities." Unpublished manuscript, National Park Service, BSFNRRA, 1981.

Hutchinson, Steven K., et al. *An Inventory and Evaluation of Architectural and Engineering Resources of the BSFNRRA.* Lexington, Ky.: Environment Consultants, Inc., 1982.

Jones, James B. *The Development of Coal Mining on Tennessee's Cumberland Plateau, 1880–1930,* Study Unit #6. Nashville, Tenn.: State Historic Preservation Office, 1987.

Manning, Russ. *The Historic Cumberland Plateau, An Explorer's Guide,* Second Edition. Knoxville, Tenn.: The University of Tennessee Press, 1999.

———. *100 Trails of the Big South Fork.* Seattle, Wash.: The Mountaineers Books, 2000.

McBride, Kim A. *A Background Archival and Oral Historical Study of the Barthell Coal Camp, McCreary County, Kentucky.* Lexington, Ky.: University of Kentucky, 1993.

National Park Service. *Roads and Trails Management Plan Draft.* BSFNRRA, 1993.

———. *A Guide to Paddling in the Big South Fork.* BSFNRRA, undated.

———. "Big South Fork National River and Recreation Area Cemetery Inventory." Unpublished report, BSFNRRA, Resource Management Division, 1989-90.

Perry, L. E. *McCreary Conquest: A Narrative History.* Whitley City, Ky.: Published by the author, 1979.

Perry, Samuel D. *South Fork Country.* Detroit: Harlo Press, 1983.

Shepherd, Russell G. "America's First Commercial Oil Well." *Earth Sciences History,* Vol. 1, No. 2 (1988): 134–139.

Smith, H. Clay. *Dusty Bits of the Forgotten Past, A History of Scott County.* Oneida, Tenn.: The Scott County Historical Society, 1985.

Stanley, Steven M. *Earth and Life Through Time.* New York: W. H. Freeman and Co., 1986.

Thomas, J. Patrick. *Lore & Legend, History Magazine,* Vol. 1, No. 1. (1989). Devoted to the history of the Stearns Coal & Lumber Company.

U.S. Army Corps of Engineers. *Structural Treatment Plan, National Register Eligible Architectural Structures, BSFNRRA.* Nashville, Tenn.: U.S. Army Corps of Engineers, 1986.

———. *Big South Fork General Design Memorandum and Final Environmental Impact Statement.* Nashville, Tenn.: U.S. Army Corps of Engineers, 1976.

Index

About the Author

Russ Manning began his career as a science writer, but for the past ten years has devoted his attention to travel and outdoor subjects. He has authored numerous books about the Southeast, including *75 Hikes in Virginia's Shenandoah National Park*; *100 Hikes in the Great Smoky Mountains National Park*; *100 Trails of the Big South Fork*; and *40 Hikes in Tennessee's South Cumberland*. He has also written over 200 articles for such magazines as *Outside*, *Backpacker*, *The Tennessee Conservationist*, *Appalachia*, and *Environmental Ethics*.

THE MOUNTAINEERS, founded in 1906, is a nonprofit outdoor activity and conservation club, whose mission is "to explore, study, preserve, and enjoy the natural beauty of the outdoors. . . ." Based in Seattle, Washington, the club is now the third-largest such organization in the United States, with 15,000 members and five branches throughout Washington State.

The Mountaineers sponsors both classes and year-round outdoor activities in the Pacific Northwest, which include hiking, mountain climbing, ski-touring, snowshoeing, bicycling, camping, kayaking and canoeing, nature study, sailing, and adventure travel. The club's conservation division supports environmental causes through educational activities, sponsoring legislation, and presenting informational programs. All club activities are led by skilled, experienced volunteers, who are dedicated to promoting safe and responsible enjoyment and preservation of the outdoors.

If you would like to participate in these organized outdoor activities or the club's programs, consider a membership in The Mountaineers. For information and an application, write or call The Mountaineers, Club Headquarters, 300 Third Avenue West, Seattle, Washington 98119; 206-284-6310.

The Mountaineers Books, an active, nonprofit publishing program of the club, produces guidebooks, instructional texts, historical works, natural history guides, and works on environmental conservation. All books produced by The Mountaineers fulfill the club's mission.

Send or call for our catalog of more than 450 outdoor titles

 The Mountaineers Books
1001 SW Klickitat Way, Suite 201
Seattle, WA 98134
800-553-4453
mbooks@mountaineers.org
www.mountaineersbooks.org